Supporting Children with Communication Problems

Sharing the Workload

Jannet A. Wright and Myra Kersner

David Fulton Publishers
London

David Fulton Publishers Ltd
Ormond House, 26–27 Boswell Street, London WC1N 3JD

First published in Great Britain by David Fulton Publishers 1998

British Library Cataloguing in Publication Data
A catalogue record for this book is available from the British Library

ISBN 1–85346–468–6

Typeset by Textype Typesetters, Cambridge
Printed in Great Britain by The Cromwell Press, Trowbridge, Wiltshire

Contents

Introduction

This book has many origins. It has arisen not only out of our own interests and areas of research, but also out of the needs of practitioners and students. In addition, it has been informed by practitioners: the practising teachers and speech and language therapists working with children with communication problems who, over the years, attended the Continuing Education Study Days run by the Department of Human Communication Science at University College London: for they shared their concerns, their questions and their ideas with us about the ways in which professionals may work together for communication impaired children. We are also indebted to the many teachers and therapists who responded to our research surveys. In addition, the book owes much to the fruitful discussions which have taken place within our own clinical practice, and when visiting students in training.

During the years we have spent supervising the postgraduate projects of practitioners we have found many teachers and therapists who were eager to gain further knowledge about ways of working together for children with communication problems. Through their research, they were seeking to relate theoretical issues to their working practice and to inform their own practices by exploring the ways in which others worked together. So often we wished that there were more books to which we could refer them – books in which these issues were explored.

Supporting Children with Communication Problems: sharing the workload is, therefore, for practising teachers and therapists who have begun to work together and wish to know more about the process, as well as for those professionals who may be considering embarking on such work but need to consider the 'pros and cons' of working in this way. It is for members of both professions who may be pursuing their continuing professional development, as it is intended that it will provide background information to the various approaches as well as discussion of the advantages and disadvantages of these approaches for teachers and speech and language therapists, as they strive to share the workload.

The book is also for student teachers and speech and language therapy students. We hope that it will be of value to them during their initial professional training, and that it will enable them to begin to understand some of the factors involved in the complex undertaking of 'working together' for children with communication problems. Of course, we hope that it may inspire them in their future professional practice.

This is not a 'how to' book, rather it is a resource book, bringing together information about the ways in which teachers and speech and language therapists are currently working together in a variety of settings. It aims to enable teachers and therapists to gain some insight into the development of working relationships so that they may consider realistically the implications of joint working practice within their own work setting.

Chapter 1 sets the scene. It introduces all aspects of the topic, providing relevant background information. Chapter 2 focuses on terminology and looks at the labels used within the literature to describe the ways in which educational and therapy professionals work together. If support is needed or arguments required in order to justify working together, these are to be found in Chapter 3. For those who wish to consider the advantages and disadvantages, pitfalls and pleasures of joint working practice, please turn to Chapter 4. Specific aspects relating to working together in individual settings are considered in separate chapters: primary and secondary mainstream schools in Chapter 5; special schools covering all school-aged children in Chapter 6; and special units, including the provision in pre-school and secondary units with specific emphasis on primary Language Units, in Chapter 7. For those who are more interested in the dynamic process of the relationship, this is explored in Chapter 8.

Jannet A. Wright and Myra Kersner
University College London
February 1998

Chapter 1

Supporting children with communication problems

Introduction

There are a range of communication problems which may affect school-aged children and these may occur for a variety of reasons. While children with such problems are within the education system, several different professionals may be involved with the identification and amelioration of their communication difficulties. These include: teachers and classroom assistants; speech and language therapists, and educational psychologists. Parents too normally play a significant and important role. However, whilst it is important to recognise this, the focus of this book will be on the interaction between the professionals; in particular, the relationship between the teachers and the speech and language therapists who work together in order to help such children.

Who are the children?

Classification – an historical perspective

The 1945 Handicapped Pupils and School Health Services Regulations listed 11 categories of handicap of children for which local education authorities were required to make special educational provision. These included: physical handicap; educationally subnormal; maladjusted; epileptic; deaf and partially deaf. Many of the children within these categories would have had associated speech and language difficulties. At the same time – and for the first time – speech defects was also recognised as a specific category.

Those children who were labelled as having speech defects and who normally attended ordinary schools were seen by the speech therapist at the local school clinic. Those attending special schools, which were designated by the primary classification of their difficulties, may have been seen by a speech therapist within their school setting. The medical approach to such difficulties was the prevailing influence at that time, when it was thought that children would be 'cured' by regular treatment from a speech therapist.

Children who were classified as mentally handicapped (or severely educationally subnormal), most of whom also had associated communication problems, were the responsibility of the local health authorities and, as such, were not automatically entitled to an education. It was not until 1971, following the implementation of the Education (Handicapped Children) Act (1970) which removed the power of health authorities who provided training for these children, that local education authorities assumed responsibility for them. All children of school age who had hitherto attended Junior Occupation Centres and Junior Training Centres were then entitled to education for the first time, although their speech therapy continued to be provided by the health authority, usually within the newly designated special schools.

Current descriptions

The 1981 Education Act changed the way in which children's problems were conceptualised. The categories of handicap were removed and there was a shift of emphasis, encouraging more descriptive reporting and classification of children's special educational needs, including their communication difficulties. It was envisaged that a description of needs would enable the education authorities to offer the most appropriate form of educational provision, and to recommend services and resources such as speech and language therapy as required. For some children this provision is recorded on a Statement of Special Educational Needs* – the current formal statutory assessment procedure. However, there are many children whose needs are currently being met without a Statement having been written.

---

*In Northern Ireland this is also referred to as a Statement of Special Educational Needs, although in Scotland it is known as a Record of Needs.

What is a 'communication problem'?

The range of communication problems

Some children who have no cognitive deficit or physical problem may be described as having a specific speech and language impairment, so identifying communication as the primary problem (this used to be referred to as developmental dysphasia). However, in many other cases, such as children with more complex needs, the speech and language problem may be a secondary aspect of their overall difficulties. For example, deaf children, children with cerebral palsy, or severe learning disabilities may have problems developing speech as well as language as a result of their medical condition or intellectual impairment. In some instances it may not be possible to distinguish which is the primary and which the secondary problem. Such may be the case where children exhibit challenging behaviour; it may not be clear whether this is the cause or the effect of the speech and language difficulty (Wintgens 1996).

For some children, their speech and language difficulty may have been identified in their pre-school years and have been resolved by the time they enter school. However an underlying difficulty may then be manifest, such as a specific learning difficulty (dyslexia) where the development of their literacy skills will be affected (Catts 1996; Stackhouse 1996).

As well as problems which may affect speech and/or language development of young children, other developmental communication problems which may be prevalent in school-aged children include dysfluency (or stuttering/stammering), and voice problems. It is also possible that children may acquire a communication problem as a result of illness or accident.

Identification of expressive problems

There are some communication problems which are easier to identify than others (MorganBarry and Wright 1996). Difficulties with expressive language which may affect the form and/or the content of what children have to say (Bloom and Lahey 1978) are usually identified more readily. For example, children's speech may be difficult to follow if they are unable to sequence sentences correctly according to acceptable English word-order, or to use appropriate grammatical structures (syntax). Similarly apparent are articulation or phonological problems, where children are not able to formulate or sequence English speech sounds correctly, or cannot use them contrastively, so reducing their intelligibility.

Children who have complex needs may not have the physical ability to produce sounds accurately or may not have the voluntary control to produce sounds at will (dysarthria and dyspraxia). In some situations such children may use alternative or augmentative communication systems (AAC) – such as a signing system (Makaton; Paget Gorman Signed Speech) or a symbol system (Rebus; Makaton Symbols; Blissymbolics) to supplement speech.

It is not always a straightforward task, however, to identify the problem when children have difficulty with semantics or the meanings of words. Such children may have intelligible speech and use syntax appropriately, but may be unable to select appropriate vocabulary or recall the names of specific objects.

Identification of pragmatic problems

Sometimes children have problems interacting and communicating with other people. This use of language (Bloom and Lahey 1978) or the development of pragmatic skills is closely intertwined with social behaviour and, whilst it may not be difficult to identify children whose social communication behaviour is 'odd', it may not always be easy to pinpoint the exact nature of the problem. The majority of children learn unconsciously how to address friends, parents and teachers in a variety of ways, all of which are socially acceptable. Children who have difficulties in this area, however, do not acquire these pragmatic skills automatically. For example, they may not know how to attract another's attention, how to initiate or end a conversation, or how to take turns when talking. Similarly, if a conversation comes to an unexpected halt due to a misunderstanding they would not know how to restart or repair it.

They may also have difficulties with non-verbal communication so that they have poor eye-contact, use gestures inappropriately or fail to appreciate culturally acceptable distances which people maintain when conversing with others.

Overall, such children may not be aware of the nuances which many people take for granted in general conversation. They may not know how to deal with vocabulary which expresses emotions and abstract concepts such as happiness or sadness, or they may not be aware of the subtle difference, for instance, between 'liking' and 'loving' people. Failure to understand the implications of specific vocabulary may mean that they find it difficult to link topics in conversation, or to talk about something or someone who is not present.

Identification of receptive problems

Difficulties with the comprehension and understanding of spoken language – 'receptive' problems are also less obvious and thus more difficult to identify, for as Wright (1995) says: 'Often, [these] can be overlooked due to the prominent nature of expressive language difficulties'. Nevertheless they may have serious consequences for children in relation to their speech and language development.

In the classroom where there are organised, predictable routines, children with comprehension problems may function unnoticed for they will make good use of non-verbal and contextually linked clues to enable them to follow instructions. Often, however, they will interpret instructions literally which can lead to difficulties, not least in understanding sarcasm and verbal humour. They may also have difficulties understanding abstract concepts, favouring concrete examples and 'real', current situations. However, the fact that they have difficulties in making inferences and predictions and in understanding the relationship between cause and effect may create potentially dangerous situations for them, for they will be unable to predict the consequences of their own or someone else's actions.

Despite their lack of comprehension, such children often have expressive language, although this will usually be limited and in-appropriate. Children who echo the teacher's – and other children's – words or whose own conversation is plentiful yet meaningless may have an underlying comprehension problem which is masked by their apparent 'chattiness'.

All these difficulties can manifest themselves in both oral and written work and have implications for the children's social and educational development and progress. Aspects of identification will be discussed in further detail in Chapter 5.

What provision is currently available?

In the wake of the 1981 Education Act, children were described as having special needs and special educational provision was made available as appropriate. According to the Code of Practice on the Identification and Assessment of Special Educational Needs (DFE 1994) special educational provision for children over the age of two means: 'educational provision which is additional to, or otherwise different from, the educational provision made generally for children of the child's age in maintained schools, other than special schools, in the area' (2.1, p. 5).

Children with communication problems will need speech and language therapy as part of this provision although, according to the Code of Practice, 'speech and language therapy may be regarded as either educational or non-educational provision depending on the health or developmental history of each child' (4:34).

The ways in which speech and language therapy is provided will in part depend on how it is recorded on the child's statement, i.e. as an educational or non-educational provision. However, speech and language therapy provision will vary from one geographical area to another, according to the way in which the speech and language therapy services are organised in the area, and dependent upon the educational setting.

Currently children with communication difficulties may be found in a variety of educational settings so that the provision offered may be at any point on a continuum, which ranges from mainstream schools in which children are either fully integrated or are supported individually in specific areas, through specialist units where children are only partially integrated, to the opposite extreme of specialist schools, where children with special needs are segregated.

The nature of the setting will not only affect the speech and language therapy service provision but also the ways in which the therapists may work; in particular how they may work together with the teachers. The fact that in some areas speech and language therapists are funded partly by the education authority whereas, more often, therapists continue to be funded predominantly by the health authority, may also affect how they work alongside teachers and function within a school. Some of these issues will be discussed below.

The different settings within which teachers and speech and language therapists may work together will be discussed in more detail in Chapters

5, 6 and 7. The effects of a communication problem will have different implications for children at different stages in their education – at pre-school, primary, or secondary stages – dependent on when the problem is first identified and whether or not it is persistent. This will also have implications for the professionals working with these children and will be discussed in other chapters.

Who are the professionals?

Some children with speech and language difficulties may have been identified at an early age, for example by a health visitor, and consequently may begin to receive speech and language therapy prior to starting school; therapy may then continue after they have entered the education system. For other children, the class teacher may be the first professional to identify their communication difficulties. The teacher will then be the one who will refer them to the speech and language therapist. Irrespective of who has the initial contact, in both situations these two professionals – the teacher and the therapist – will need to bring together their knowledge and skills in order that the communication difficulties are addressed and the children in their care may benefit.

How then may a professional partnership result in educational plans for children with communication problems? And how may speech and language therapy be incorporated into the requirements of the National Curriculum? In order to understand how this may be achieved, it is important to look at the individual roles of each of these professionals; to examine their training; and to consider some of the factors which may affect the ways in which they may work together.

Teachers – roles and ways of working

In mainstream schools, teachers are responsible for the education of the children, which includes the delivery of the National Curriculum. The ways in which individual schools are organised will vary according to the size of the school and its overall structure. Naturally, there will be some differences in teachers' roles and the ways in which they work within individual schools. However, there are significant differences between the role of the classroom teachers in primary schools and their role in secondary schools. This may be important when considering teachers who work with children with communication problems, for it may affect their approach to working with such children.

Primary teachers have responsibility for all subject areas, even where individual teachers within a school may be responsible for staff development within a specific subject area. This means that primary teachers normally maintain contact with all the children in their class for most of the working day, including children with communication problems or other special educational needs. However, in secondary schools all teachers have a subject specialism and work within departments. They normally focus on their subject area, teaching across years and within years where ability groups will vary considerably. Their contact with individual children, therefore, may be minimal, unless they have the additional role of form tutor, or are involved in the pastoral care of the children.

The departmental structure and the large number of students who attend the majority of secondary schools will mean that the management and organisation of the secondary school will differ greatly from that of most primary schools, which generally have smaller numbers of staff and students. Indeed, secondary schools will often have a special needs department as well as designated staff who provide pastoral care. This, therefore, creates a network of subject teachers, support staff and staff on pastoral care teams all of whom will need to liaise together in order to help children with special educational needs, including children with communication problems (Miller and Roux 1997).

In larger primary or secondary, mainstream schools children with such problems may be catered for by a learning support team, often led by the special educational needs coordinator (SENCO). In smaller schools, the SENCO will be more directly involved in the special educational provision. The SENCO has the overall responsibility within a school to maintain the appropriate records, and coordinate the special provision for the children with special educational needs, which will include children with speech and language problems, in line with the school's policy. This may involve working with specific children either in the classroom or on a withdrawal basis. In addition, it is the responsibility of the SENCO to liaise with, train and advise the staff of the school, and to liaise with parents and any external agencies which may be involved with the children (Stage 2; Code of Practice 1994). However, in many primary schools, the SENCO will also have a teaching commitment for part of the week, which naturally reduces the time available for the specialist role.

Class teachers in a mainstream school may have an additional role – as managers. There may be many different adults involved in classroom activities during the course of a week. Such adults may include non-teaching assistants, parents, volunteers or teachers in training, as well as support workers such as the SENCO or external advisory teachers. If there are children in the class who have communication problems, the speech and language therapist may also be a regular visitor. It is the class teachers who have the overall responsibility for the organisation and management of all those working within their classroom and, where other professionals are involved, they have additional responsibilities. Not only must the teachers ensure that their own class-based tasks are completed so that the pupils may continue to learn and function effectively but, through careful negotiation and liaison, they need to ensure that the professional needs and requirements of their visitors are also met.

At the same time, when planning their own and the children's timetable, teachers have to take into consideration the academic cycle of events which are part of the school calendar. Educationally orientated events such as termly reports, annual reviews, standardised assessment tasks (SATs) and individual education plans (IEPs) all impinge on the school timetable, as well as important social events on the calendar such as the annual festivals which are usually celebrated by a school as a whole and require many hours of practice and preparation.

These, of course, are part of the working life of all teachers although, in more segregated, specialist schools and units where any of the classroom teachers may be involved with children with special needs and communication problems, the roles and duties of the teachers may vary from those of teachers in mainstream schools. Like the teachers in mainstream schools they are responsible for delivery of the curriculum. In special schools, however, the curriculum modification which is necessary for any children with special educational needs will be required for all the children in each of the classes.

One of the other specific differences relates to the size of the classes. In specialist schools or units the classes are usually smaller than in mainstream schools, and normally there is a lower student to staff ratio. However, this often means that there are even more adults for the class teacher to manage. In the specialist setting, non-teaching assistants, classroom volunteers and a range of health service professionals will normally work in the classroom on a regular basis as this is often essential in order to facilitate and enable small group activities. Opportunities for whole-class activities are often limited due to the diverse – and sometimes extreme – nature of the difficulties some of the children may experience and this may only be possible by careful classroom management and by greatly reducing the student to staff ratio.

In order for teachers to be able to organise and manage their classroom effectively, and for children to benefit from the specialist work, it is important for teachers to be as knowledgeable as possible about the type of problems experienced by the children with whom they work. Indeed, whether through qualification or classroom experience, teachers working in such specialist settings often have specialist knowledge about the needs of the children they teach, even though this is not a statutory requirement.

Teachers' training

Initial teacher training (ITT) has varied greatly over the years so that in the modern classroom a teacher may have any one of a number of different qualifications including, a certificate of education, a specialist subject degree coupled with a teaching diploma, an educationally focused degree or a classroom based training (Fleming *et al.* 1997). Similarly, within each school, teachers may have a variety of additional qualifications. Although in some specialist settings it is mandatory for a teacher to have a special additional qualification, such as for those working with children with sensory impairment, teachers who work with children with communication problems do not necessarily need a specialist qualification in speech and language difficulties.

Many teachers who trained in the 1970s and early 1980s will have had some special educational needs input in their initial training for, as Kersner (1996) points out, 'from the early 1970s many of the standard 3 and 4 year initial teacher training courses began to incorporate special education . . . into their syllabuses'. The incorporation of this specialist training in ITT was phased out by 1986, to be replaced by in-service training offered by the LEAs, although this did not result in the same number of teachers receiving specialist training (Miller and Porter 1994).

The Education Act (1988) had a further impact on ITT as there was a 'diminution of time available for subsidiary subjects and other themes which could be regarded as background issues to a student's general training in education. One such theme ... [was] the issue of special educational needs' (Garner 1994). However, since the 1993 Education Act and the 1994 Code of Practice imposes a legal requirement on teachers to monitor and record the progress of pupils, it would seem to be important that teacher training should prepare teachers for these responsibilities. Towards this end, in 1995 a Special Educational Needs Training Consortium (SENTC) working party reviewed 'the systems currently in place for the training of teachers of pupils with special educational needs ... [and made] recommendations on how these systems might be improved to make efficient and/or effective use of resources in light of the respective roles and responsibilities of those involved in the provision of special educational needs teacher training' (SENTC 1996). One of these recommendations was that teachers responsible for pupils with special educational needs should be required to reach an appropriate level of competence which may include recognised qualifications. Individual working groups then produced a list of competencies which were seen as basic requirements for teachers working in specific areas of special educational needs.

The following competencies were identified for those working with children with speech and language difficulties.

1. Teachers should be able to make observations which reflect knowledge and understanding of the processes of communication and language within the overall development of the children.
2. Teachers should be able to recognise the nature of communication and language difficulties and their effects on children's learning.
3. Teachers should be able to plan, implement and evaluate the curriculum taking into account the needs of children with communication and language difficulties.
4. Teachers should be able to participate in and evaluate interprofessional intervention with children with communication and language difficulties.
5. Teachers should be able to reflect on their own spoken and written communication skills with children and their parents and with colleagues.

6. Teachers should be able to reflect on their own teaching practice and describe any changes they have made as a result of their study.

(Miller and Wright 1995, p. 312–13).

Despite the fact that they are not mandatory, at the time of going to press, there are some specific additional qualifications currently available for teachers working with children with communication problems. Apart from the variety of short courses, which are offered either through in-service training or through higher educational establishments, several award bearing courses are available for qualified teachers. These are offered by the education departments of different universities on a full- or part-time basis as well as through distance learning (see Chapter 7), and they deal specifically with the speech, language and communication difficulties of school-aged children.

Therapists – roles and ways of working

Speech and language therapists are required to take on several different roles in the work place. They may be called upon to act as trainers, advisors or as multidisciplinary or interdisciplinary team members, as well as offering speech and language therapy – specific counselling and therapy to individuals or small groups of clients. In addition, they may work in many different ways, their patterns of service delivery having changed over time. These may vary according to different circumstances including geographical location, type of setting – and length of waiting lists.

The majority of speech and language therapists who work with children are employed by the National Health Service (NHS), and they follow the standards and guidelines for practice laid down by the Royal College of Speech and Language Therapists (RCSLT) which are currently documented in Communicating Quality (RCSLT 1996). This has been the case since the Reorganisation of the Health Service Act (1973) which saw the school health service merge with the NHS. Historically, therefore, this meant that therapists tended to be based in clinics so that they have had little opportunity to work directly with teachers in mainstream schools. Following the 1973 Act, however, the new speech and language therapy career structure enabled therapists to develop different areas of specialisation, often with senior therapists being made responsible for a specialist team. Therefore, in special schools at least, therapists began to work alongside the teaching staff and were able to develop their own specialist knowledge.

It was the Education Acts of 1981 and 1988 which next had a significant impact on the ways in which speech and language therapists worked with children, and since the implementation of these Acts there have been many changes in the patterns of service delivery. The 1996 Education Act has since enabled many of these changes to be consolidated. As more children with special educational needs were integrated into mainstream schools, so posts were created within speech and language therapy services enabling therapists to support children with communication problems – children with and without statements – in those mainstream schools.

The organisation of speech and language therapy services providing this support varies from one geographic location to another. Some speech and language therapists are now employed by education authorities, working only within schools, and in some areas this has led to the creation of a separate service for mainstream schools, one at primary level and one at secondary level. This potentially increases the opportunities for teachers and therapists to work together so that children with communication problems may find that their therapy and academic work becomes more integrated. For despite the fact that speech and language therapists offer children with communication problems 'therapy', the needs of the majority of children with special educational needs must be considered as 'educational' (RCSLT 1997).

In other areas there are still children in mainstream schools who receive speech and language therapy at a local health centre, where the speech and language therapist continues to work alongside other health service professionals. In such instances it is not surprising if parents coming to such a centre are influenced by the medically orientated setting and perceive the speech and language therapy which their child is receiving as separate from his or her education. Indeed, it is more difficult to integrate therapy which is provided in this way with the child's education as the therapist will need to make a specific school visit in order to meet with the teacher. In a study by Wright (1994) it was often newly qualified therapists who were based in health centres. Roux (1996) however reports that this is now changing as in some areas newly qualified therapists are being specifically encouraged to work in mainstream schools.

There will be many therapists who, despite being responsible for providing a service to several mainstream schools for children with communication problems, maintain their administrative base at a health centre. If they spend a significant amount of time in each school they will have more opportunities to discuss the educational implications with the teachers as well as work with the children, thus possibly pre-empting the potential risk of educational failure for the children. However, they will need to arrange specific times when they can visit the schools in order to support the children and to meet with the class teachers, and the frequency of the visits to each individual school may vary greatly, as will the length of each individual session with the children. This variability of session length and frequency of attendance may also apply to children who have to visit the health centre.

There are different pressures on individual speech and language therapists dependent upon their work location and setting, and this was confirmed in a research study by Wright (1994). Some therapists prefer to be based in health centres for, if they are not spending a large part of the day travelling between locations, they can see more children and thus reduce their waiting lists. However, it is possible, on occasion, that children seen in health centres could be discharged from therapy prematurely. They may have improved to the point of developing adequate coping strategies for the one-to-one situation within the clinic, although it is possible that these strategies are masking the children's inability to generalise the improved communication skills to the classroom at school. For this and other reasons, teachers generally prefer it if children are seen by the therapists within the school environment. Teachers usually view therapists' visits to the schools as preferable to the children having to miss half a day of lessons in order to attend a session at a health centre. From the therapists' point of view, one of the positive aspects about visiting the school is that there is less possibility of children not attending therapy sessions.

Therapists' training

There are currently two primary routes to qualification as a speech and language therapist: at undergraduate level, via a three or four year degree course; or through two years of intensive study at postgraduate level. 'All speech and language therapy training is accredited by the RCSLT and is generic in nature' (Kersner 1996), so that all graduates are qualified to work with both adults and children who have communication problems. However, each course will have its own distinctive orientation so that, for example, one may be more medically biased in its approach, while another will emphasise the linguistic approach. Understanding the role of the teacher and the education system within which the children are situated will normally be included in the syllabus of all courses. However, the weighting given to this area of study will vary for each course.

Although therapists are not expected to develop a specialism until after they have qualified, there are only a limited number of opportunities available for speech and language therapists to achieve additional specialist qualifications. Since the early 1980s a small number of Advanced Clinical Studies courses, accredited by the professional body, have been available. This means that therapists could become specialists, for example in working with deaf people, or in working with people with severe learning disabilities. However, the only post qualification courses available for speech and language therapists enabling them to learn more about the teacher's role, the education system and children with special educational needs are run through in-service training (INSET), or through the short continuing education courses which may be provided by various higher education establishments. These are rarely award bearing courses. Nevertheless, as with teachers, it is possible for therapists to become more specialised in working with this client group by virtue of their years of practical work experience with children with special educational needs.

Dual qualification

There are an increasing number of people who are dually qualified – as a teacher and as a speech and language therapist. However, as Newman (1996) points out, teachers and therapists each have a different role with children and a different philosophy of language which will affect the ways in which they work. Therefore, although such a dual qualification will help to provide an individual with insight into both professions, it is rare for one person to act as both therapist and class teacher to the children.

Working together – sharing the workload

There are many different factors which will affect how teachers and therapists work together, not least of which are the differences in roles, ways of working and training outlined above. In addition, there are external organisational factors which affect both professions. Recent changes in the health service mean that therapists are facing the new 'market forces' in much the same way as teachers and heads of schools are coming to terms with the implications of current legislation.

Speech and language therapy services which offered a unified service across education and health are now being split into smaller units, each focussing on a more specialised area such as acute services and community provision. Primary financial constraints and limitation of resources often force therapists to develop a pattern of service delivery based on a specific number of contacts or sessions, irrespective of an individual child's needs. In addition, the management of such services may no longer be the responsibility of someone from the same professional group, and this can have a profound effect on an individual therapist's working patterns and affect opportunities for professional development (see Chapter 4).

Teachers have been required to make similar adjustments to their working lives. For example, with the introduction of the National Curriculum (Education Reform Act 1988) and the local management of (special) schools (LMS and LMSS), teachers are often now required to cope with financial budgeting, as well as the changes in curriculum content, delivery and classroom management.

However, the changes in the legislation since the 1980s has meant that teachers and therapists now have more opportunities to work together, although the additional roles and expectations placed on both professionals will have an impact on the ways in which this may happen. In the current climate of increasing pressure to market individual professions as schools and services are each in competition with others, and the constant expectation of increased productivity, the demands on both professionals are considerable. It is not an easy time to develop working partnerships and yet, paradoxically, it may be through such partnerships that children with communication problems can most benefit and that the individual professionals may have opportunities to grow and develop professionally. Individually neither teachers nor therapists are in a position to instigate change, nor to influence any of the changes which have been thrust upon them. Together they may be in a strong position to influence their immediate working environment to their mutual benefit as well as for the benefit of the children.

However, the fact that there are more opportunities for two professionals to be in more regular contact does not mean that they will automatically develop a close working partnership (Wright 1994; Graham 1995). In order to enable this, as more opportunities arise for joint working practice – not only in special units and schools but also in mainstream schools – it becomes increasingly important for each to reconceptualise the therapists' roles within the schools, to recognise their differences and to establish common, or at least complementary, approaches so that they may develop ways in which they may work together in order to benefit children with communication difficulties.

How their differences may be reconciled, compromises be negotiated and partnerships developed in order to share the workload will be discussed in the following chapters.

Chapter 2

Sharing the workload –
models of working practice

Introduction

The phrase 'working together' may be used to describe people who merely work alongside each other, or it could be taken to mean something more specific. This depends upon whether those who are working together form a dyad – two people working as a partnership, or whether they are part of a team of people; and whether the partners, or team members, are from the same or different professions. Within the context of this book, as indicated in the previous chapter, it is the shared, dyadic working relationship between teachers and therapists working with children with communication problems which is under scrutiny. The ways in which they work together for the benefit of the children, their professional relationship, and their interdependence within that partnership will also be discussed.

The importance of working together is generally accepted by professionals. Indeed, pooling resources, expertise and a specific part of the workload by working together becomes an extremely effective way of using the limited human resources available with regard to working with such children. This is particularly relevant as it seems unlikely that there will ever be enough teachers with specialist speech and language qualifications to cope with the numbers of children in the classroom with communication problems. Similarly, it is improbable that there will ever be sufficient therapists within local health or education authorities to meet the needs of all the school-aged children who have speech and language difficulties. Kersner and Wright (1995) suggested that working together may be one of the best ways of meeting the needs of children with communication problems as it enables the professionals to share their professional expertise. The use of their combined skills is likely to be more cost and time effective in relation to the children's progress than if they both worked individually and in isolation.

One of the advantages when two different professionals work together is that, through the differences in their training (see Chapter 1), the teachers and the therapists who form this pairing are able to bring unique and special professional skills to their work situation and thus to the working partnership. For example, teachers are specifically skilled in classroom management; working with large as well as small groups; teaching reading and number work, and approaching language through the broad categories of speaking and listening; and reading, writing and spelling, as required by the National Curriculum. Their assessment approach will be based on the children's cognitive skills. They take a holistic approach to the children's ability to function and work within the constraints of the classroom coupled with their knowledge of the children's home and social background.

Therapists' skills lie in their ability to assess children's understanding of language and to analyse their spoken language. They consider in detail the articulation and phonological processes used, the syntax, the levels of vocabulary and semantics, as well as the children's functional and social use of language. Therapists, through their phonetics and linguistic training, are skilled at pinpointing where and why a breakdown in language and speech development has occurred. A therapist's holistic view will include focusing on the children's medical as well as social development, so that any physical and/or medical disability which may be contributing to the children's communication difficulties will be taken into consideration, as well as environmental problems.

Within different teacher–therapist partnerships there will be different permutations and combinations of expertise. For example, it may be that in one pair both of the individuals are specialists with regard to children with special educational needs, either by virtue of additional qualifications, or through their years of specific working experience. Within another pair, one may be considered to be a specialist, either by qualification or by experience, while the other may be relatively new to working with children with such problems. Whatever the combination, in each unique pairing different aspects of the specific expertise of each of the individuals will be highlighted and it is generally accepted that the professional knowledge and skills of each of them will be maximised when they are pooled.

Working together is also endorsed by the professional organisations. For example, the RCSLT acknowledge that 'a mainstream service where the speech and language therapist and education staff work together will improve communication and increase opportunities for sharing expertise' (RCSLT 1996). They go on to recommend that services should be delivered 'in such a way as to enable education staff to incorporate the aims of speech and language therapy in the planning of the language programme in the context of the broad curriculum'. In the USA, the professional body for speech and language pathologists, the American Speech-Hearing Association (ASHA), also recommends that teachers and speech and language therapists should work together in schools. For, as they point out, 'no one professional has an adequate knowledge base or expertise to execute all the functions associated with providing educational services for students' (ASHA 1991).

When considering how the workload may be shared between such professionals who are employed mainly within the health and education systems it is important to consider how the different ways in which they work together may be conceptualised, for this will be described variously in different and even similar contexts.

The use of labels

The ways in which teachers and therapists work together – the models of working practice – are generally referred to by specific labels so that terms such as 'collaboration', 'partnership', 'consultation' (among others) are to be found in the literature. However, although these terms are commonly used in North American and antipodean literature as well as in the UK to describe patterns of joint working practice in the educational system, they often mean different things to different people. This is because, despite the fact that they have been endowed with a specific technical meaning within a given context, these labels, in addition, are regular English words. As such, their technical usage may be arbitrary, and they may be used interchangeably without reference to their technical definition even within a specific context. Thus, for example, when describing the working patterns of some teachers and therapists 'the word "collaboration" is often used interchangeably with "co-operation", to denote harmonious working together' (Roberts 1994), although their approach may not conform for example with Idol and West's (1991) definition of collaboration which includes 'parity and reciprocity'. Naturally, this can lead to confusion in practice if the more colloquial connotation rather than the definitive usage is taken to be the meaning.

Such potential confusion, however, should not preclude the use of labels. They may still be a useful method of descriptive shorthand – for example, describing the ways in which people work without the process having to be explained in full. Obviously, to avoid confusion it is helpful if the label is defined within the context in which it is used.

In order to understand some of the technical distinctions which are often made between the different dyadic relationships referred to in this book, some of the most common labels which are used to describe different models of working practice will be discussed below.

The effects of using labels

Before describing the labels themselves, it is important to consider how such labels, when they are attached to a professional's way of working, will directly affect the ways in which others – professional colleagues, outside agencies, or parents – perceive that work; for the use of specific labels will lead to expectations being raised about the professionals and their approach, and the possible outcome of the work. When the labels are applied by the individuals themselves about their working methods, it also means that they are making a statement about their own perceptions of their work and this will affect their own expectations of themselves, and of others in relation to themselves within that role. For example, if,teachers say that they are working 'in cooperation' with each other, this will convey messages about what they will expect of themselves and how they will expect to work. It will also provide the basis for others' understanding about what may be expected of the individuals, the partnership, and/or the service offered.

In this way, the labels given to different types of partnerships will provide a framework within which the professionals may work. For example, if teaching staff within a school say that they work 'collaboratively', then this will raise the expectations of a visiting therapist about how the staff function as a group and how they may relate to a colleague from a different profession who is working within the school.

Of course, the ways in which any group of teachers, or teachers and therapists, will work together is dependent on many factors within the work setting such as the potential opportunities for meeting in order to work together, their previous professional experience, and their experience of working closely with colleagues. However, despite these factors the initial expectation is raised and set as soon as a key descriptive label is used.

Labelling the models

Consultation

The term 'consultant' is not at this moment a profession-specific 'protected' title, but the consultation model of working practice is more traditionally associated with medical professionals rather than with educationalists. Although it is now also a common business and commercial label, particularly in relation to finance, the term consultant is perhaps most commonly used as a title to indicate a senior medical practitioner, a specialist in a particular field of medicine whose opinion is sought by both professional colleagues and patients. Expectations arising from such a title or label are such that when patients attend a hospital appointment to see the Consultant they will be disappointed if they are seen by another medical officer. No matter how knowledgeable the Registrar or Senior Registrar is within the medical hierarchy, the patients' perceptions will usually be that such a person is, nevertheless, junior to the Consultant. Thus patients will feel that they are not receiving attention from the 'specialist', the most knowledgeable person in the team.

The term consultant or specific derivations of the word such as consultation, carry an implicit message not only about the Consultant – the person – and his or her approach, but also about the role of the consultee. The level of responsibility which each party would be expected to take (and would themselves expect to take) is implied by the use of this specific label. That is, the consultee will present a 'problem' which is perceived to be within the area of the consultant's specialist expertise. The consultant will gather further information and then attempt to solve or reduce the problem by making suggestions or recommendations which the consultee is then responsible for implementing. There is no expectation in this interaction that a more active participatory role will be taken by the consultee. Thus the consultative approach sets up the consultant as the 'expert'.

This relates to a model described by Cunningham and Davis (1985) when they identified common ways of working between non-medical professionals and parents of children experiencing difficulties. They described one of the models as 'The Expert Model', where the label 'expert' is synonymous with 'consultant'. Thus, in the same way, parents would expect the professionals to have the knowledge and expertise to solve the educational, social and developmental problems of their child; and they would expect to be told what to do. Equally, the professionals would expect to be deferred to by the parents and would expect parents to carry out their suggestions and recommendations.

In such a situation parents may have a set period of time such as six to eight weeks before meeting with the consultant again to review the child's progress. In practice, this period may prove to be too long. Almond (1997), as the mother of a child with severe communication problems, describes feeling 'abandoned' when offered this pattern of service delivery. She reports that other parents also found that 'the quick chat once a month' left them feeling unsupported, and they would have preferred more frequent contact with more active therapist involvement.

It is possible that the same feelings could occur if the label 'expert' or 'consultant' which has been applied to the ways in which patient and doctors, or parents and professionals, may interact together, is used to describe the ways in which pairs of other health or education professionals relate to each other as they work together. In such a dyad, if one professional is seen as having greater knowledge and expertise than the other, then the two are likely to interact in their working relationship as if one were in the role of consultant and the other consultee. However, the consultee may experience similar feelings of 'abandonment' if the time period between meetings is too long.

In addition, this way of working does suggest a professional hierarchy which does not necessarily allow for the development of an equal partnership. There is little scope within this model for there to be 'give and take' between the professionals and it is possible that this could lead to a dependency on the expert by the one who is considered to be less knowledgeable. Ultimately this could lead to over-dependency. Such an issue was highlighted by Norwich (1990) when he pointed out that if speech and language therapy services are offered to schools on a consultative basis so that the role of the teachers or assistants is to work directly with the children on activities which have been suggested by the therapist, then this will lead to teachers being dependent on the therapists. Thus they may perceive themselves to be in a subordinate position to the therapists.

Idol and West (1987), working in the USA, also acknowledge that a consultative approach has traditionally meant that the consultee maintains a dependence on the consultant. Nevertheless, they view consultation in a positive light so that, for example, they would recommend that teachers in mainstream settings should seek the support and advice of the specialist teachers, specifically because of the fact that they are the ones with the specialist knowledge. The suggestion is then that the aim of consultation in a school setting should be for the specialist teachers to help class teachers to solve current problems so that the class teachers will gain sufficient knowledge to be able to approach similar problems in the future by themselves. Thus, in the long term, the consultee's dependency on the consultant will be reduced (Idol and West 1987).

The North American researchers Conoley and Conoley (1992) also see this as the aim of consultation which they define as a 'voluntary, non-supervisory relationship between professionals from differing fields designed to aid professional functioning'. They too suggest that the consultee may generalise to other clients the special knowledge and skills which they have learnt in relation to the problems of one specific client. In this way a teacher who consults with a therapist or a learning support teacher about a child with specific learning difficulties may find that the activities suggested for this child may be used equally successfully with other children in the classroom.

Similarly, Figg and Stoker (1989), when writing about the working relationships between educational psychologists and teachers in the UK which they describe as 'consultative', suggest that it is not unreasonable to expect the consultee to learn from the consultant in such a relationship. The teachers as the consultee are usually responsible for implementing recommendations following a consultation with the educational psychologists. Jordan (1994) suggests that there are four stages in this consultation process, beginning with the contracting stage where roles and parameters are established as well as agreed needs and expectations. This is followed by the development of a plan of action, a reporting and feedback stage, and finally an evaluation of the outcome.

However, it is important during this process for the teachers not to feel deskilled, unable to deal with difficult situations and particular problems. For, as the teachers become more skilled, they should be able to build on the advice received from the 'consultant' and dependence on the psychologists should diminish.

In an educational setting, it is possible that the term 'advisor' may be more appropriately applied to a speech and language therapist or specialist teacher who works with others who are less knowledgeable in specific relation to speech and language difficulties. For not only is this another way in which the consultative role may be perceived, but also the label itself may be more acceptable. Indeed, in the UK when SENCOs work with class teachers, they are more likely to be referred to as advisors rather than consultants even though, usually, they are working in a consultative way. In the Wright study (1994), speech and language therapists indicated that teachers contacted them 'for advice' about children who were unintelligible; 'for advice' about strategies for managing such children in the classroom; and 'for advice and help' relating to general concerns regarding communication. The role of advisor may be the same as that of consultant but the change of label will have a significant effect, in terms of connotations, perceptions and expectations.

Similarly, if the teacher or therapist in the consulting role is referred to as a 'resource' it will affect the way in which the role is perceived. The role is still consultative but implicit in the label is the fact that the specialist has specific knowledge, skills and contacts which any teacher or professional colleague may draw on when working with children who have speech and language difficulties. The use of such a label as a 'resource person' may also be more acceptable within the education system, and this may lead more conducively to the development of a 'give and take' relationship between the professionals concerned.

Collaboration

The label 'collaboration' is one of the most frequently used terms in the context of professionals working together. However, its use is rarely constrained by any specific definition, for it may be used to describe approaches ranging from fluid, loose-knit networking to intensive joint working practice. Reid *et al.* (1996) state that in their report on teachers' and therapists' work in Scotland, 'collaboration' is used as an 'umbrella term' to cover 'all types of situations in which a professional works jointly with, liaises with or otherwise includes other people who are in a client's environment in order to achieve educational or speech and language therapy aims'. This may include 'direct face-to-face work with a client or indirect input to, or manipulation of, the client's environment'.

However, many other authors when writing about collaborative work are more specific in their definition. For example, Loxley (1997), when describing interprofessional collaboration, describes it as a process of 'relating across boundaries given the differences between the professions. It is a device for managing and organising resources and a technique for delivering services'. Others stress the sharing nature of the working relationship which develops between the professionals. There is an expectation of 'give and take', mutuality and support, and a two directional flow of information, advice and help. For example in North America, collaborative working has been described as 'sharing the work and responsibility for some activity' (Conoley and Conoley 1992); and as 'two or more professionals working together with parity and reciprocity to solve problems' (Idol and West 1991). The 'egalitarian' aspect of the relationship was also described in the earlier work of Conoley and Conoley (1982). Similarly in the UK, Lacey (1996) feels that 'collaboration involves a willingness on the part of individuals to share expertise, plan jointly, work alongside each other, exchange roles and support each other completely'.

Roberts (1994) feels that 'it refers to the particular situation where a group of people come to work together because of their membership in other groups . . . whose tasks overlap'. Collaboration may then enable them to carry out the task more effectively.

Working collaboratively does not mean that each aspect of the work is necessarily covered by both members of the dyad. Indeed, one of the positive advantages of such a working relationship must be that joint decisions may be taken about the division of labour. Each of the individuals will then bring different strengths and expertise to the work, so that each may be involved in different aspects of its implementation. In practice, this may mean for example that one pairing may decide that mutually agreed goals should be individually implemented; whereas in a different pairing the reverse may be more appropriate, as was found in a study by Wright (1994).

In Wright's study the speech and language therapists said that they worked collaboratively with the teachers in order to implement the intervention strategies for the children's speech and language problems. However, these strategies were based on the findings of assessments which had been carried out by the therapists alone, and the resultant treatment plans which had also been drawn up by the therapists unilaterally. Although, in this instance, it may not have been appropriate for the teachers to take part in the assessment process, it must be recognised that unless the professionals are able to plan an intervention strategy together there is a risk of reducing the coherence of the approach to the children's overall needs.

Where the teachers and therapists were jointly involved in the assessment of children with communication difficulties, as reported by Kersner and Wright (1996) in their study of teachers' and therapists' joint working practices in special schools, it was suggested that the teachers showed a greater commitment to working with the therapists regarding the planning and implementation of the intervention strategy than had been found by Wright (1994). The commitment was such that a large proportion of teachers said that they, or their non-teaching assistants, continued the therapy even in the absence of the therapist. In this study the teachers and therapists who were working with children with severe learning disabilities (SLD) demonstrated a high level of collaborative working practice. It is possible, however, that the teachers in such settings felt more comfortable being involved in the work of the therapists because of their own specialist knowledge which may have given them a greater understanding of what the therapists were trying to achieve.

One approach to collaboration, which has been developed by Dale (1996) in relation to professionals working with parents, is called 'The Negotiating Model', where the 'negotiation' between the professionals and parents is the key transaction in the shared work. This model developed out of the belief that both parents and professionals have independent, yet potentially valuable contributions to offer children with special needs. The approach to the working relationship is that 'partners use negotiation and joint decision making and resolve differences of opinion and disagreement, in order to reach some kind of shared perspective or jointly agreed decision on issues of mutual concern' (Dale 1996). Naturally, such a model may also be applied to many different situations, so that it would seem appropriate to use it to describe the ways in which many dyads of professionals would work together in order to achieve a collaborative relationship. Thus, for example, where a therapist may lack the confidence to work within the classroom, and the teacher's arrangements for specific language lessons are dependent on a requisite number of adults being in the classroom, including the therapist, the two will have to resolve their differences, negotiating perhaps one session a week initially as a trial period.

Collaborative consultation

One of the labels which is less frequently used in the UK to describe joint working practice is the term 'collaborative consultation' which has its origins in the work of Johnson *et al.* (1990). From their work and other similar literature from the USA it would seem that there has been an attempt to link the term 'collaboration' with 'consultation' in order to reflect the equality of status of those who may be working together. Johnson *et al.* suggest that collaboration where people work together on an equal footing has its roots in the consultation model, but they use the combination of terms as a label in order to suggest greater parity between the individuals working together than is normally implied by the term 'consultant', as described above.

Cooperation

Axelrod in 1984 put forward his 'Cooperation Theory' when considering ways in which people work together. He suggested that all parties who use this approach cooperate for their own benefit – for what was later referred to by Loxley (1997) as 'a mutual overall gain'. The term 'cooperation' implies that professionals 'work alongside' each other without reference to a status conflict or struggle for maintenance of a power balance within the relationship. However, it is important that no one individual of a pair or team becomes too dominant in a cooperative relationship as this could lead to coercion of others during decision-making processes. A model of good practice of the cooperative approach has been described by Idol and West (1991) as one where 'two or more parties, each with separate and autonomous programmes, agree to work together in making all such programmes more successful'. Naturally, this will have important implications within a classroom setting where teachers and therapists are both working with communication impaired children.

There are many different situations within the education system where professionals may find it helpful to work together cooperatively in order to benefit children with communication problems, either as full members of a team, or alongside an existing team. One example may be in senior mainstream schools where the visiting speech and language therapists will need to try to work cooperatively with the SENCOs and/or members of the schools' learning support teams. In such instances the therapists may be full team members, or co-opted members, working with the existing team only in relation to specific children. Another example may be in primary mainstream schools where the professionals may be in a dyadic relationship. In such instances the teachers and therapists may be unable to work more closely together because of time or other constraints. However, they may agree at least to try to forge cooperative links in order to ensure that the children's therapy programmes and progress within the classroom are equally maintained.

According to 'co-operative theory', in a cooperative partnership professionals' working relationships are not as close knit nor as interdependent as in collaborative, or even consultative, pairings. Thus it is not so critical for the dyads, or larger groupings, to reflect closely on the development and process of their working relationships. Neither is it necessary for the individuals to maintain close contact or constant communication, so long as workable contact is maintained and the lines of communication are kept open. In many instances this is all that is possible between busy teachers and therapists who are trying to work together regarding specific children's communication problems. This was clearly demonstrated in Wright's research (1994) which indicated that the most commonly convened meetings between the teachers and therapists who were surveyed lasted for a maximum of ten minutes, and these had to be snatched at break times, lunchtime or after school when the children were no longer there.

Teamwork

As the term implies, teamwork involves more than two professionals working together at any one time. Some teams may develop by default, for example because of the number of professionals who happen to be involved in specific and related issues. More often, teams are brought together specifically so that they may work together on common, shared tasks; for as Lacey and Lomas (1993) point out, 'Effective teamwork can lead to better service provision, increased energy and progression and greater job satisfaction. A well co-ordinated team can in many cases lead to better use of individual skills.'

Thus, in interdisciplinary or multidisciplinary teams where the members all come from different professions, the main aim will be to pool knowledge and reach decisions collectively. The hope is that as all the specialists' skills are brought together in this way, under one roof, this will lead to the provision of an effective coordinated service.

However, within a mainstream school setting interdisciplinary teams may have an imbalance of representatives across professions. For example, a learning support team will consist mostly of teachers, with possible individual representation by an educational psychologist and a speech and language therapist. In special schools it is more likely that other professionals such as those engaged in physiotherapy, occupational therapy, social work and clinical psychology may be represented. A senior medical officer is also likely to be a team member. Naturally, the constitution of the membership will affect how the team approach their task and function collectively.

As may be expected, therefore, working in a team will not automatically result in close cooperation, and attempts to work collaboratively within a team may not be successful. Multidisciplinary teams in reality, because of their wide cross-professional representation often 'have difficulty developing a cohesive and shared common purpose, since their members come from different trainings with different values, priorities and preoccupations' (Roberts 1994). Despite the fact that task oriented teams have a defined common purpose and that the team membership is determined by the requirements of the task so that each member has a specific contribution to make, in a multidisciplinary team there is still the potential for the members to act more like a 'collection of individuals', so that interdisciplinary fights and rivalries may be restimulated, resulting in a failure to coordinate and progress their activities (Roberts 1994).

However, whilst close collaborative work may not be possible within the framework of a multidisciplinary team, there is nevertheless a wealth of expertise and specialist skills within any team of professionals. Through their shared common interest and concern for the children in their care, normally such teams are able to pool their knowledge and work together so that important decisions are reached at least cooperatively.

Labelling used within this book

In order to avoid confusion between the different labels and the ways in which they may be used, throughout this book we shall refer to the working relationship between pairs of teachers and therapists as 'working together', describing in each instance, as relevant, the nature of the relationship in terms of the levels of cooperation, collaboration or consultation, and the pertinent consequences which may result from such methods of working together.

The advantages and disadvantages of working together in some of the different ways described above will be further discussed in Chapter 3.

Chapter 3

Why work together?

Introduction

There are numerous examples of references to teachers and speech and language therapists who have always worked together in respect of the communication impaired children in their care, as discussed in Chapter 1 (Kersner and Wright 1996; Wright 1994; Lacey and Lomas 1993). To date, this has more traditionally been the case in special schools and language or special resource units. However, recently there have been many external factors which have forced teachers, therapists and other professionals who have not previously worked together to consider new ways of thinking with regard to their working practice.

Within the education system these factors include changes in curriculum content, new and different methods of delivering the curriculum, responsibility for the school financial budget and the need to 'sell' the school in the 'market place'. Factors in the NHS include changes in Trusts in terms of responsibility and fund-holding, and the introduction of GP fund-holding. In addition, the changes in service delivery offered by speech and language therapists working with communication impaired children, particularly in mainstream schools, has meant that many more mainstream teachers and therapists are having to consider more effective ways of using their time so that their work is maximised and not merely duplicated. As five per cent of children enter school with difficulties in speech and language (RCSLT Leaflet RC97L) it is apparent that there are larger numbers than ever of children requiring help.

As a result, many more professionals have begun to consider new ways in which they may work together. Initially working together seemed to be mainly of benefit to the professionals as a way of reducing their stress levels, and indeed for their own survival. For, as a survey among therapists in the NHS showed (Kersner and Stone 1990), many speech and language therapists found being able to talk to and work with colleagues helped them to cope with their stress, and support from colleagues made them more effective in their work. Similarly it has been shown that teachers find that sharing problems with a colleague can be a way of reducing stress, and that supportive relationships at work may be a useful coping strategy (Dunham 1992). However, many professionals have since found that working together is helpful not only for their own well being, but also for the children's ultimate benefit and have begun to seek ways in which they may continue to develop this aspect of their work.

Thus, within the education system, many teachers have begun to think about the ways in which they have liaised and worked with members of support services in the past and to consider possible changes which they may wish to make in their approach in the future. For example, as a result of one of the developments relating to the National Curriculum, teachers now have to take responsibility for conducting assessments such as standard assessment tasks (SATs). This has meant that often teachers have to reorganise and reprioritise their work. Even if they have an allocation of non-contact time this is usually limited and they may have to consider redistributing their time during the working day. This would include the time available for working with the professionals who offer support services, such as speech and language therapists. In many instances it is factors such as this which have led to teachers and speech and language therapists seeking to develop their working relationships in order to work more effectively as a pair, for they realise that together they may achieve results which, independently, neither of them will be in a position to achieve.

Where both parties instinctively recognise the benefits of working together, the actual approach adopted by the working partnership may 'just happen' without either party specifically addressing the issue with the other. However, it cannot be assumed that strong working links will be forged automatically, nor that discernibly positive working patterns will be immediately apparent. Often, teachers and therapists find that their relationships evolve over time as they improve their professional acquaintance for, even where the formation of the dyad is deliberate and considered, it takes time for productive working relationships to develop. The closeness of the relationship and whether the partnership is cooperative, consultative, or collaborative in approach will depend on many factors which will vary according to each specific situation.

In some cases, the development of professional partnerships may be part of the school ethos and thus within that school there will be an expectation that visiting professionals from support services, who are not available on a full time basis to the individual school, will work together with the teachers. In other cases, one or other of the professionals may have to take the initiative in order for a partnership to develop. Whatever the background situation, the nature of the working relationship will be dependent on the professionals concerned.

It will be incumbent on the therapists to consider which model of service delivery may be most effective for individual children, and for the teachers to decide what service may ideally be required within the specific classroom. It will then be the joint responsibility of the teachers and therapists to consider how they may best function together in the interests of the children, and how they may make maximum use of all additional classroom help which may be available, for example from classroom assistants, and will include a consideration of the importance of the development of language in relation to curriculum requirements.

The need to work together

The centrality of language

One of the major factors underlying the specific need for teachers and speech and language therapists to work together is the significance of language in children's development, and in particular its importance in relation to all aspects of their development during their years at school. For not only does 'healthy' speech and language development underpin the acquisition of reading, spelling and literacy skills (Catts 1996; Stackhouse 1996) but, in mainstream schools, language (through speech) is also the medium of instruction for all aspects of academic – and non-academic – teaching and learning. It is central to most aspects of the National Curriculum, as well as being the normally preferred medium for social communication. It is important therefore to ensure that children have every opportunity to develop their speech and language skills to their maximum potential so that they may optimise all the learning opportunities presented to them during their school years, and so that they may function ultimately as full and accepted members of society.

Consequently, help must be offered to children who experience difficulties, such as delayed or disordered language and/or speech, in order to facilitate all aspects of their development. Within a school setting the most effective form of help is usually that which is offered not in isolation but which is related to the children's immediate social and educational environment. This will mean that even if children are withdrawn from the classroom for individual therapy therapists must forge links with the teachers so that individual work may be carried over into the classroom in some way. This will increase the children's motivation and encourage generalisation of any new language acquired in therapy to the naturalistic setting of the classroom, thereby making it more meaningful.

In order to achieve this, it is important for there to be a strong working relationship between the teachers and the speech and language therapists and for them both to understand the interdependency between language and learning. This will then enable them to facilitate the children's development of language in relation to curriculum requirements, and in relation to everyday needs, so that the children will be adequately equipped to follow instructions and receive information related to everyday events in the classroom and the school.

Language and the curriculum

In the early years of their education the majority of children begin to understand concepts of size, colour, number, shape, and the meaning of time: past, present and future (Winyard 1996). The associated vocabulary is understood and used meaningfully around the same time. Such concept formation and linguistic development provides the foundation on which much of their later education is based. It follows therefore that, without this basic understanding and the words with which to describe their new knowledge, children will have difficulty grappling with many of their subsequent curriculum subjects. Such is often the case for children who have communication problems. Many children who have inherent language difficulties, which are not related to a significant cognitive deficit, may continue to struggle educationally throughout their school careers.

In addition, there is a strong corpus of research evidence indicating that children who have difficulties with the development of early language skills are 'at risk' regarding their literacy development. Many such children have been found to have difficulties in acquiring literacy competence, even where their oral speech and language development has improved to an acceptable standard, as there is thought to be an underlying deficit affecting all aspects of their speech and language development. (For further reading see Snowling and Stackhouse 1996.)

As problems which may occur at different levels of linguistic functioning will have varying effects on children's learning, it is important to distinguish between verbal comprehension and expressive language. As discussed in Chapter 1, expressive difficulties are normally easy to detect, for example when children are trying to respond to questions in class; during 'show and tell' or 'circle time', or if children are taking part in any form of debate or discussion. Problems with expression may be due to grammatical or phonological difficulties.

However, even though other language difficulties may not be so overtly apparent they may, nevertheless, prove to be handicapping for children. For example, in class, children with receptive problems may interpret explanations or instructions literally, often with understandably disastrous consequences. Thus, when being told to 'pull their socks up' such children may be seen to bend down and adjust their socks: often to the amusement of their peers! With other children, even though their speech and language may be developing, there may be subtle 'higher linguistic levels' of difficulty so that they may have problems making and understanding inferences, making predictions, or recognising the relationship between cause and effect. This may mean that, as the children progress through school and curriculum subjects become more abstract, for example in English, Chemistry, or even History and Geography, children with such problems may become less able to cope.

Another less obvious difficulty which may nonetheless prove to be a handicap is a specific word-finding disorder. In any curriculum subject children need to be able to understand and use the vocabulary related to specific subjects. These children, however, despite having intelligible, grammatical speech, will have a specific problem finding the appropriate word, or will have difficulty remembering vocabulary. It is important to recognise such children in the classroom so that repetition of the target words and appropriate modification of the curriculum may be made to enable them to learn the new words.

There are also evidence based links between language and the development of arithmetical and mathematical skills (Donlan 1992), and the ways in which a language deficit may affect the development of numeracy in children will need to be considered.

Thus it can be seen that the development of speech and language is fundamental to children's progress at school. The children's needs in terms of achievement related to the National Curriculum must therefore be a major consideration of any speech and language therapy programme. Normally, this can best be achieved through the combined knowledge and skills of the professionals involved.

Social use of language

The other major area for consideration regarding therapy is for children to be able to function adequately with the social demands of school life, for this too may prove problematic for children with speech and language difficulties. Once again, the nature of the potential problems for children with expressive, or even some receptive language difficulties may be obvious. However, children who have problems with their pragmatic skills, who may be able to cope generally with the academic aspects of the curriculum, may not understand the social aspects and use of language. Consequently they may find it hard to take part in group activities, or to mix easily with their peers. For example, such children may have difficulties indicating that they want to take a turn to speak; they may not know how to initiate or end a conversation, nor how to ask questions. Thus they may not be able to ask appropriate questions in order to clarify their confusion, so that they may not be sure how to continue with or complete a given activity or task in the classroom. In such cases, teachers and therapists will need to work together to ensure that the children in their class have every opportunity to become adequately socially competent and well-adjusted.

Language without speech

Of course, in some special schools, speech may not be the sole means of communication, and in such specialised settings therapists are often able to offer information and advice on specific aspects of communication such as AAC systems (see Chapter 1). For example, some children with physical disabilities may use symbol systems, or computers, as a means of expressing their language, just as some of those who have a hearing impairment may use sign language as their primary medium of expression. Children with severe learning disabilities may use some combination of simple signs and/or symbols to augment, or replace, their speech. Speech and language therapists normally have specific expertise regarding AAC systems. Indeed, Kersner (1996) found that teachers working with children who had either severe learning difficulties or particularly constraining physical handicaps, felt that the therapists they worked with had specific information and skills which they needed to share, not only about signing and symbol systems, but also about feeding and swallowing techniques. Thus, it seems particularly important that where children are dependent on alternative systems, teachers and therapists work together so that they may choose an appropriate system, implement and maintain the use of the system, and ensure continuity of use of the system, between therapy, school and home, so that the children have consistent ease of access to communication.

The rationale for working together

Working together in any of the situations outlined above means that there is an economy of time and effort required from the professionals involved. For by working together they will be able to reduce the amount of repetition and overlap which could result if they were forced to work in isolation. Therapy can be streamlined and continuity ensured if, for example, there is joint involvement in the speech and language assessment process. Then, joint planning of therapy in relation to children's IEPs can ensure that the children's needs are met comprehensively and that plans for intervention are fully cohesive, increasing the amount and quality of 'therapy type time' which the children are able to receive (Fleming *et al.* 1997). It would not be too strong a statement to say that in some settings, unless the therapist can find a way of working with and through the teachers, it may be impossible to provide an adequate service for the children.

A theoretical approach to working together

A combined working approach – as with any developing partnership – requires compromise, and the individuals concerned will naturally perceive that there are positive as well as negative aspects to their working relationship. There may prove to be many advantages for both parties in terms of personal job satisfaction and professional development. However, there may also be some perceived disadvantages to working together.

Blau (1986) in his Social Exchange Theory suggests that when people engage in an interaction they continually assess their personal gains and losses which result from the exchange. Naturally, they expect to achieve more gains, or profits, than losses and if this occurs then it will perpetuate the interaction. This means, therefore, that when working together, the professionals will only continue if both of them are continually rewarded by their joint working practice, assuming that they will be able to make clearly explicit to each other what they see as the benefits of working together.

The disadvantages of working together

According to the Contact Hypothesis (Sherif 1966), professionals may become more positive about each other as they spend time together, working towards a common goal. However, it is important to take a realistic approach to the development of joint working patterns. If, from the beginning, the two professionals are able to recognise and acknowledge some of the disadvantages of working together as well as the benefits then, as the partnership develops, they will be able to consider ways in which they may work to overcome them.

One of the major drawbacks, referred to by the majority of respondents in research surveys undertaken by the authors (Wright 1994: Kersner and Wright 1995) is *time*: the amount of time required in order to make joint working practice effective. Respondents in both studies referred to the difficulties of finding the time to talk together – and the stress this inevitably causes; finding the time to plan activities; finding the time to implement either the activities which had been specifically designated as 'therapy', or activities which were considered to be part of the continuity of the therapy programme within the classroom.

For the teacher, the need to meet regularly with another professional may feel like 'yet another thing they have to do'. Classroom teachers not only have to take responsibility for the class, its organisation, timetable and teaching, but have to make themselves available equally to the children and other adults who may work in the classroom. This all adds to teachers' general levels of stress (Dunham 1992). Having to liaise and share information with yet another professional (the speech and language therapist) may seem like an unacceptable extra task. In addition, some of the adults who work in the classroom on a regular basis may show resentment at what they may perceive as the monopolisation of 'their' teacher by another professional.

The daily schedule is no less pressurised for the therapists. The time they have to spend in each individual school is usually limited and therapists often have difficulty in organising all their required meetings with teachers, and sometimes even with the children, due to the many conflicting activities which occur within the school during the course of an average day.

If designated discussion time is allowed for within the school timetable, during the working day, then Mills (1996) suggests that this is an indication of how the head teacher values the contact between the professionals. It may be seen as a measure of the commitment of the school management to the development of joint working practice.

Some negative aspects of working together are more related to personal feelings, such as the propriety felt by many professionals in relation to their specific skills and knowledge. Conscious of their own strengths and the areas in which they may be more specifically qualified or experienced, they may be unwilling to undertake anything which they do not see as being directly related to their own area of expertise. They may feel irritated at having to do what they see as 'someone else's job'. On the other hand, there are some professionals who resent having to share with others what they feel to be their area of speciality, for fear of 'losing the mystery' or 'the professional magic' (Wright 1994). They cannot make compromises as they are unable to see that it is possible for each to bring their own particular strengths to the situation. They fear that by working closely together they are deskilling themselves, enabling the other to do their job, and it is not surprising, therefore, that they are reluctant to share information and skills.

It has been argued that by working together within a consultative framework (see Chapter 2) the consultants ultimately may no longer be needed, for as they pass on their own skills, they themselves become redundant. Speech and language therapists for example, invited to take a consultative role, may feel threatened, fearful of 'losing' their skills, of 'giving them away'. Their automatic response in such cases to the negative feelings would be to try to ensure that the teachers do not gain too much knowledge or skill relating to speech and language therapy. This however is a narrow and largely unrealistic viewpoint. However informed and skilled the teachers may become at dealing with specific problems, they do not automatically become experts themselves in speech and language therapy, any more than the therapists could take the place of the teachers. For there is not a finite set of skills or knowledge which diminishes each time they are shared with another. While each is able to work in a more informed way because of the new knowledge they have gained, different problems will continue to arise which will still require the other's expertise.

What is perhaps more important when two professionals work together is the delicate balance which must be achieved with regard to each acknowledging the knowledge and skills of the other and the ability to share those skills. For, without that, it is possible that one or other of the pair could feel professionally vulnerable as they expose what they feel to be their 'professional ignorance' when working together, and this may leave them feeling deskilled. For example, it is possible that some teachers may feel that as the speech and language therapists are the experts on speech and language, they (the therapists) should be the ones dealing solely with that aspect of the work with the children. At the same time the therapists may feel that because the teachers are with the children most of the day, in a naturalistic setting, they are best placed to carry out the speech and language therapy programme.

This then may lead to one of the most difficult questions which arises in any such working relationship where both of the professionals have their own specific areas of expertise: who takes the lead? Both teachers and speech and language therapists enjoy a degree of autonomy in relation to their work and it may be that neither is willing to give up any part of this autonomy for fear of losing control of their own working situation. Inevitably there will have to be some degree of compromise in order that a comfortable working relationship may develop. However, it may be that both are still reluctant to take the initiative in the new partnership for fear of being seen as 'leader'. One specific difficulty in relation to this, particularly in mainstream schools, is the inequality of status. Generally the therapist is the visitor or guest in the school, whereas the teacher is usually a permanent member of staff, and this may lead to some initial unease in the relationship as the two work through the process of balancing the power, their autonomy, the workload and their respective roles.

Of course sometimes there may be practical disadvantages to teachers and therapists working closely together which may not have been considered by either of the pair. For example, therapists who are fully integrated into the schools' reviews procedures would naturally expect to be present at annual review sessions, particularly of statemented children. However if all reviews are carried out at a specific time of year, the implications of the speech and language therapist's unavailablity to work with the children during this block of time may not have been considered. Ultimately, technological advances such as video conferencing may help to solve such difficulties, but currently this is only of limited availability.

However, whilst acknowledging the disadvantages of working together, it is important to say that these are possibly outweighed by the many advantages which result from joint working practice. Indeed, the teachers and therapists in the Wright study (1994) and the Kersner and Wright survey (1996) had no difficulties in listing what they saw as the benefits gained, as discussed below.

The advantages of working together

Benefits for the professionals

When any two people work together, the result is often more productive than the sum of the work which they could have produced individually. There is an economy of time and effort – a more effective use of time in order to meet the children's needs. There is the generation of new and creative ideas which often results from the stimulation each offers the other in a dynamic working relationship. They can brainstorm ideas together and 'bounce ideas' off each other, and they can listen to each other so that, as referred to in terms of action research (Edwards and Talbot 1994), one takes the role of 'critical friend' during the course of planning and evaluating sessions. This may enable both of the professionals to become more reflective in their practice.

This in turn may lead to mutual support and the creation of opportunities for sharing concerns. The effects of receiving support from a professional colleague cannot be underestimated for, as shown in the Kersner and Stone NHS study (1990) and reported for teachers by Dunham (1992), such support helps to reduce stress at work. Not only is it important to offer, and receive, help and suggestions about children who are not making progress or who are difficult to manage, but also to provide affirmation when things are going well. All professionals value the opportunity to share with colleagues their professional successes, particularly concerning children with special needs whose progress may be very slow: and they recognise as well the need for a chance to share their periods of professional uncertainty.

Working together has important implications for continuing professional development, and there are benefits to be gained by both of the professionals concerned. One of the most interesting findings identified in the Wright (1994) study was the fact that the teachers and speech and language therapists who worked together found that they learnt so much from each other. Because they each had trained in different ways and because they worked in different ways, they had much complementary knowledge and skills to pool. The later study (Kersner and Wright 1996) similarly showed that teachers and therapists were able to find ways in which they could share their expertise effectively, for their mutual benefit, without professional detriment to either of them. The respondents in that study felt that some of the information was gained incidentally. For example, the therapists learned about classroom organisation, watched teachers controlling groups of children, and gleaned much background information about the general behaviour and performance of individual children. Through having the complementary perspective of their colleague each of the professionals was able to attain a more holistic view of the children with whom they were working.

Other knowledge was acquired more explicitly through sharing of specific, specialist skills so that, for example, the teachers learned about signing systems and communication aids from the therapists; and the therapists gained knowledge about reading schemes. In a good working partnership this information and skills exchange will be ongoing, as views continue to be aired and shared and new aspects of knowledge are constantly being gained by both parties.

By working more closely together, the teachers and therapists usually find that they are able to develop a better understanding and appreciation of each others' roles which consequently enables them to see new ways in which they may work together in order to maximise their complementary skills and knowledge. Thus teachers may become more aware of how speech and language problems may affect children's performance in the classroom, and develop strategies to help them cope with the effect of the language deficit on their numeracy and literacy development. At the same time teachers may become more confident in their ability to recognise which problems are appropriate for referral to the therapist. Therapists, on the other hand, may become more adept at structuring their therapy to make it relevant to the children's classroom experience so that the naturalistic setting of the classroom can provide the appropriate environment in which carry-over and generalisation of the therapy may continue outside of the specific therapy sessions.

As well as understanding each others' roles, if teachers and therapists work closely together it may also help other colleagues to understand more about their work. For example, being associated with specific teachers within a school may enable a visiting therapist to become more quickly established as part of the special needs team within that school. The SENCO and the other teachers will have an immediate point of reference and this may enable them to develop a greater understanding of the role of the therapist. In Wright's study (1994) some therapists referred to working together as 'a means of self-preservation', the only means through which they felt they could achieve results within a particular school. Others referred to working together as a means of enabling them to become more quickly a 'part of the system' in which they would be working.

Even on a practical level, there may be benefits to joint working practices. Working closely with a teacher may provide an 'anchor', a 'place to be', so obviating the need for a specifically designated room, which, in many cases, is not always readily available.

Not only are there benefits when working with other colleagues in the school, but also when working with parents or outside agencies, for example at annual review sessions or placement meetings. As Jowett and Evans (1996) found in their study of collaboration, two professionals working closely together may support parents more effectively than a single professional working in isolation with children.

From the parents' perspective

It is helpful not only for the teachers and therapists to feel that they have each others' support, but also for the parents to see that the professionals are pooling their knowledge and expertise for the benefit of their child. When a health service professional is able to work with children within the educational setting, it must be obvious to parents that the children are receiving a coordinated input for their special needs rather than fragmented provision. Parents whose children have their communication problems identified once they start school often assume therapy will be provided in school. They may also have the expectation that the therapist will personally carry out all therapy face-to-face even though this may not be possible. However, if parents understand the importance of speech, language and communication within education, and can see that the teachers and therapists are working together to help children's speech and language development, then some of their anxieties about their own child may be effectively reduced.

Parents of children whose speech and language problems were identified before school entry may have attended therapy sessions at a health centre or a Child Development Centre. This takes up much time, often involving difficult journeys (as highlighted by Reid *et al.* 1996 in their study in Scotland), and places additional demands on other family members. It is naturally helpful to parents if the therapy service can be offered in school when children reach school age and, when making choices about their child's future educational placement, they may view more favourably schools which offer speech and language therapy services on site; this may include therapists who are based at the school, or therapists who at least visit regularly to work with the children. However, it may also include schools where therapists do not visit frequently but work closely with and through the teachers and assistants within the classroom.

Benefits for the children

Of course it is the benefit derived by the children from the speech and language therapy services offered which will ultimately influence parental decisions regarding therapy options, and possibly choice of schools.

There are many ways in which children with communication problems may benefit from the joint working practice of the professionals involved. For example, if the aims regarding communication remediation and development are included in the children's IEPs then it is immediately apparent to all those concerned that the children's speech and language development is considered to be an integral part of their overall education programme, a critical factor in terms of children's potential development (see Chapter 2).

Such aims are more likely to be included if the teachers have been involved with the speech and language therapists in the assessment of the children's speech and language abilities, so that joint goals have been identified which both professionals can work towards. This will not only indicate to the parents that the child's speech and language therapy has been placed within the educational framework, but also that all aspects of the children's communication will be included within curricular activities, a factor which can only be of benefit for the children. For, as Kersner and Wright suggested (1996), teachers who are involved in the assessment process appear to be more committed to involvement with children's therapy programmes, so ensuring greater continuity of approach and carry-over of therapy into naturalistic settings. If the children are encouraged not to perceive speech and language therapy and school work as 'separate' and opportunities are provided throughout the whole school day for the development and improvement of communication and language skills, rather than merely the times spent on specific spoken English curricular activities, then it may become easier for them to change their defective communication patterns.

Another specific advantage of a joint working approach within a school is that it may not then be necessary for children to be withdrawn from the classroom for individual therapy sessions; sessions which they may perceive as being unrelated to other aspects of their school work. Indeed, in some schools it is contrary to the school policy regarding support for children with special educational needs to withdraw children from the classroom for individual work. It may be that there are occasions when it is necessary, and indeed preferable, for speech and language therapy to be conducted separately, outside of the classroom, for example if the child is disruptive, or if they are being disturbed by the other children in the classroom, but this does make it more difficult for children to generalise to the classroom situation any knowledge and skills that they may have acquired in therapy. For some children, especially as they become older, being 'singled out' by withdrawal for individual work may prove to be counter-productive. Normally, it is more beneficial if the speech and language work is integrated into the classroom so that the children remain part of the whole class, rather than being treated differently.

Because therapists working in Health or Community Centres may be restricted by Trust policy concerning the number of times they may see each of the children, the reduced individual therapist/child contact time which occurs when therapy is continued in the classroom means that effectively, where appropriate, children may be able to receive more intensive therapy over an extended time period. In addition, within the classroom the teacher (and/or the therapist and whoever else is working with the children) will be able to make their therapy relevant within a variety of contexts, and specifically agreed aspects may be highlighted in different ways at different times, as appropriate. Even where therapy is carried out by the therapist individually with children, such as in Wright's study (1994) where many of the speech and language therapists were based in health centres, working with teachers enabled the therapists to ensure that the therapy carried out in the clinic was integrated into the children's school life. The therapists in the study acknowledged that the teachers who spent 'the majority of their time with a child during his waking hours' were best placed to 'reinforce things being learned in a session'. This is supported by the work of Prelock et al. (1995) in the USA, who suggest that it is irrelevant to try to develop children's vocabulary out of the context of the classroom.

There are ultimately a limited number of hours that either teachers or therapists can spend with the children who have communication problems and it is to the children's benefit if the hours available are used to maximum effect.

Chapter 4

Factors influencing a shared professional relationship

Introduction

In a working relationship between members of two different professional groups both parties need to feel that they can benefit in order for the relationship to be maintained. According to Social Exchange Theory, as referred to in Chapter 3, if the partners feel that there is something to be gained as a result of the exchange then they are generally encouraged to continue to develop the interaction (Blau 1986). This does not preclude the differences of opinion, differences of approach and different ways of working which may occur, some of which may even result in difficulties arising when two people begin to work together. However, so long as these differences are addressed and the problems, where possible, are satisfactorily resolved then there is still the potential for the working relationship to flourish and develop.

In this chapter, some of the factors which may potentially lead to such difficulties within a professional partnership will be highlighted and discussed.

The employer – National Health Service versus Education Authority

As referred to in Chapter 1, teachers and therapists are usually employed by different statutory bodies. Teachers are normally employed by an education authority while therapists, although they may be employed by an education authority, more usually work within the NHS. In some specific cases they may have a contract through a charitable organisation. The employing agency is naturally an influential factor which will affect the ways in which the professionals work and, where professionals who are working closely together are employed by different agencies, this will inevitably have an effect on the ways in which they interact.

Implications for the children

The question of who is the employer not only affects the professionals but also has implications for the children, albeit indirectly, and the time in the children's lives when this is most critical is when they first begin to attend school. There are many children whose communication problems are identified before school entry so that initially they become the responsibility of the health service, probably visiting the speech and language therapist at the health or community centre. However, 'at the age of 5 they suddenly become the exclusive province of the educational establishment and not that of health' (Dick 1994), so that once they start attending school, speech and language therapy service provision changes.

This is not without its emotional as well as practical consequences. For example, on the part of the therapist, feelings such as 'ownership' and loyalty to the client may arise and these must be acknowledged. Therapists find suddenly that they are having to 'share' the children, that they no longer have the sole responsibility for their progress. They have to consider what they feel should be the teachers' role in the therapy process and the development of the children's speech and language. The children in turn may also experience the feeling of being shared, and at times may feel a divided loyalty between the professionals.

Implications for the parents

This major event of school entry also affects the parents, as the responsibility for the children's special needs moves out of the jurisdiction of health and into education, although it may have differing effects in different situations. For example, some parents may have expended much time and energy supporting their child through a pre-school therapy programme designed by the speech and language therapist in order that communication difficulties should not hinder their child in relation to school entry. Once accepted into the mainstream system the parents may then assume that the child is now 'better' and that any residual difficulties will automatically be dealt with by the teachers. Continuing speech and language therapy and the importance of the role of the speech and language therapist then diminishes in importance for that family.

For other families, however, it may be that the role of the therapist remains paramount, that the parents view the speech and language therapist as the 'health professional' responsible for the well-being of their child and consequently as the only person who is able to deliver therapy. Such parents may see health and education as separate entities and thus be unwilling for any teacher to become involved in their child's communication difficulties, as discussed in Chapter 3.

Research by Sandow, Stafford and Stafford (1987) showed that speech and language therapists were regarded more positively than any other professional, apart from teachers, by parents of children with special educational needs; so it may be that school entry presents a difficult time for parents of children who have been receiving therapy, as they may feel that they are losing some of the closeness of their contact with the therapist. They may not be able to understand immediately the therapy/education overlap nor to see how the teacher and therapist may be able to work together, sharing either the responsibility or the work for the remediation of their child. Of course, the policy of each school in respect of parental involvement will influence the patterns of future interactions and, in some cases, if a professional partnership is to work successfully, education of the parents in this regard may become as important as the education of the children.

There may be some sensitive issues between the teachers and therapists which will also need to be addressed and resolved in order for a successful professional partnership to develop. For example, if there has been a strong pre-existing relationship between parent and therapist the teacher may feel excluded when the child comes into school. There may not be any straightforward resolutions to such issues for, if there are confidential matters which have previously been shared by the parents which the therapist is not able to pass on to the teacher, feelings of exclusion may justifiably persist.

The reverse situation may occur when children are seen by therapists for the first time when they enter school, where it may not be easy for the therapists to meet with the parents at all. Therapists may find that they have to attend school events such as open days or coffee mornings in order to initiate links with parents, events which would not normally be part of their working schedule.

Parental contact may of course be easier to achieve in some specialist placements, particularly if the therapists are members of the school staff. Then, for example, it may even be possible for the teachers and therapists to make joint visits to the home prior to a child's school admittance.

The effects of funding the professionals – 'he who pays the piper . . .'

Professionals are naturally 'controlled' by the agency which pays their salary in so far as their contractual obligations, pay and conditions are predetermined by that funding body. Where two professionals work closely together, the fact that they are funded by two different statutory bodies will impact on the ways in which this may occur. Their working patterns will be affected in many predictable ways, such as by the fact that each will be paid according to a different pay scale, irrespective of the fact that their work will be at a comparable level.

Similarly there may be differences in the numbers of hours each is paid to work each week, and the number of extracurricular hours which they will be 'expected' to work outside of their contractual commitment. There will be differences in the number of weeks of paid holidays available and the specified times when these may be taken. Thus, for example, it is important for teachers to understand that often therapists are expected to take holidays outside of school term times because of other commitments within their own contracts; just as it is important for therapists not to resent the fact that the teachers will normally have longer holidays than therapists as this is an integral part of their contracts.

However, there may also be effects on a professional working relationship arising from the difference in employers which may not at first be so obviously apparent. As discussed in Chapter 3, one of the most difficult aspects of working together which both teachers and therapists have expressed is concerning the constraints of time, and the problems encountered in finding the time to meet to discuss the children and their difficulties. The two professionals may each have different contractual obligations regarding how they spend their time; they will have different commitments and there will be different expectations even beyond those written into their contracts.

For example, for teachers there will be specified time for student contact. In addition, there will be specific expectations with regard to assessment and marking, classroom planning and preparation which they will be expected to fulfil; assistants, support workers and students whom they may be expected to organise and supervise, and meetings such as general staff meetings which they will be expected to attend. The therapists equally will have additional commitments such as: team meetings with other therapists in their district; case review meetings with colleagues from other professions; meetings with parents; the supervision of junior therapists or students; report back meetings with senior therapists, as well as work on other sites in which they may be involved regularly. These factors not only make it physically difficult for teachers and therapists to find a mutually convenient time to meet, but may also provide fuel for potential resentments which may then smoulder if each does not understand the contractual requirements and commitments of the other's job.

However, although the amount of time they are able to spend in any one school may be limited, the nature of the therapists' work may afford them a degree of flexibility which is not so readily available to the classroom teacher. It is encouraging to note that in Wright's study (1994) 95 per cent of the therapists surveyed who were not based in a school said that they had been able to negotiate time, between ten minutes and an hour, within the school day to meet with the teachers of children with communication problems with whom they were working.

The expectations of their respective employers with regard to the reported and recorded results of their work will also be different for each of the two professionals. Class teachers for example have a set number of children within their class each year which normally remains constant throughout that school year; the results of their effectiveness will be evaluated in relation to the children's attainments on assessments such as SATs or public examinations, rather than to the numbers of children they have worked with. Similarly, although the numbers of children which support-teachers or SENCOs may be asked to see or assess will vary, the children requiring specialist help can only be generated from the given number of children within that school.

Speech and language therapists on the other hand have to produce statistics regarding the total number of children with whom they work across all their clinics and schools and, consequently, are generally required to see as many children as possible throughout each working day.

If they are NHS employees, they are bound by the NHS Patients' Charter which often means that they are under pressure to reduce waiting lists and see children within a given period from the time of their referral. The authorities who employ speech and language therapists usually measure the outcome of the therapists' work in relation to the numbers of children seen and subsequently discharged. This naturally will influence the ways in which therapists will work, as well as having an effect on factors such as the amount of time available apart from client-contact time.

The effects of funding the children

The differences in funding between the education system and the NHS not only affects the professionals, but may also have a direct effect on the children. The question regarding which statutory body is responsible for resourcing a statemented child's special educational needs is often a contentious one, but the answer may affect the level of service which is offered to a child. For example, if speech and language therapy is seen as an educational requirement and is written into section 3 of the Statement, then the ultimate responsibility for procuring and financing speech and language therapy falls to the education authority; whereas, if it is included under section 5, then the health service is responsible for the provision. The ruling in relation to Harrow LEA (in 1996) confirms that any provision allocated in a Statement of Special Educational Needs is the responsibility of the LEA even if the local health authority (HA) has failed to provide appropriate resources, but this does not make the issue less contentious if neither the LEA nor the HA has sufficient funding available.

Differences within the workplace

The place
Unless therapists are employed by a specific school to work solely within that school, they may be based in one of several different locations. For example, they may be based within one school while working in several different schools; or they may be based in a health or community centre while working in other centres and/or schools. Naturally, this will affect

the service offered both in terms of when and how often they are able to see the children, and this will have implications for how they may work with their teacher colleagues.

If therapists work solely within one school, contact with teachers will be comparatively easy and it could be either the teacher or the therapist who makes the initial approach. If they are not based in schools, therapists would normally be expected to take the initiative and make contact with the teachers of any children with whom they are working in their clinic. This of course may prove difficult for therapists whose clients attend a variety of schools or nurseries. In Wright's study (1994) 62 per cent of the therapists questioned who were clinic based said that routinely they did make such contact. However, as there were 38 per cent for whom this was not a routine part of their work, it implies that many therapists, for whatever reason, are not in a position to work closely with the classroom teachers about children whom they are seeing for therapy. As discussed previously, this has implications for the continuity of the therapy and thus possibly for the rate at which some children may be expected to improve.

Of course, even where a therapist works within one school solely, it does not mean that links will automatically be formed with all the teachers in that school who work with speech and language disordered children. If it is a large school and there are many children requiring help – all of whom are in different classes – it may take time for the therapist to establish links with relevant teachers across the school. This task may prove particularly difficult for newly qualified therapists who will be prioritising their work and their case-load for the first time in what may be an unfamiliar setting (Roux 1996). It is also possible that by the time some children reach the top of a particularly long waiting list, they have moved into a different class, and the teacher who made the initial referral for the child may not be the one who will now need to work with the therapist.

In some instances, it may not be part of the school ethos to foster close working relationships between teachers and visiting professionals. Then there may be an automatic expectation that the children will be withdrawn from the classroom for therapy and that the teacher will not be involved in the therapy process. This may prove to be a particularly difficult obstacle to a teacher and therapist who would like to work together. However, if the therapist is able to work within the classroom, this is bound to be more conducive to the development of successful joint working practices, irrespective of the school culture.

The space

The ways in which a therapist works within a school may be governed by the facilities which are offered by the school and these may vary greatly. To some extent what is offered may reflect, albeit inadvertently, how a school regards and values the therapy work undertaken. In some schools for example, a visiting professional may be offered an administrative base with telephone access and a 'pigeon-hole' for messages in the staffroom, so encouraging communication with other members of staff. However, there are disadvantages to having a specifically designated 'therapy room', for this may serve to increase the expectation that children will be withdrawn for therapy from the classroom, so proving counter-productive to the development of dynamic working relationships.

However, there are circumstances when it may be beneficial for therapy to be conducted outside of the classroom, for example when working with children who have attention difficulties who are easily distracted. Also, many therapists try to work with small groups of children who share similar communication difficulties, thus enabling the children to experience models of communication within a social setting. In such instances it may prove less disruptive if the group is run in a separate room. A specific room would also be required if the children in the group were drawn from different classes.

A health centre based therapist also faces a number of difficulties in relation to working with teachers, even though the specific obstacles may be of a different nature from those referred to above. The size of the average case-load for most speech and language therapists in clinics means that there is little time left, or flexibility within the timetable, for the development of good working relationships with colleagues on a different site. It is possible that the therapist and the teacher may never meet if the children are seen at a clinic outside of the school – indeed this may happen even if the children remain on site but are always withdrawn to a different room within the school! Neither is regular contact by telephone an easy aim to achieve. Teachers do not normally have access to a telephone while they are in the classroom, and the consecutive appointments schedule which comprises most speech and language therapists' days means that they too have little flexibility or availability to forge telecommunication links.

It is important to realise therefore that, however limited the time together, if the therapist is able to work for some of the time within the classroom this at least ensures that some verbal exchange between the teacher and therapist will take place. Of course, there can never be 'enough' time. This then makes it critical that any time spent together is fully utilised for the mutual benefit of both professionals so that there is a two-way flow of communication and information about the children concerned.

Status and role

Within a mainstream school setting there is normally a difference in status between teachers and therapists and this too will affect working patterns. The teacher is usually the permanent full time member of staff while the therapist, at best, may be a part time 'visitor' with no allegiance to, or specific knowledge of, the institution or any other staff members. Some therapists may take personal responsibility for finding out more about the schools in which they work and so become more committed to the staff with whom they find themselves working, but this would not necessarily be an aspect of their working remit which is specified by their therapy manager.

In relation to the children, it is the teachers, naturally, who are the consistent adults with whom they interact constantly in a variety of situations and settings throughout the school week. The therapists on the other hand are the 'strangers', the visitors whom the children may or may not recognise or remember well, and with whom it will normally take time to develop relationships.

Of course, the same may not apply to special schools or specialist units where therapists may not only be in attendance more often, but may even be full time members of staff. Then they have the opportunity to become fully integrated with other staff members so that, for example, they will be expected to join the children at lunch times and possibly be part of a duty rota for observation in the playground. They will be available for formal meetings and there will be more opportunities for informal, spontaneous meetings and discussions. Being part of the school in such a way presents a natural and ideal opportunity for therapists to become involved in school activities and encourages the development of closer working relationships between the teacher/therapist colleagues.

Aspects of working together which relate specifically to working in each of the different settings will be discussed in more detail in Chapters 5, 6 and 7.

Prioritising and selection – a difference of approach

Another area where misunderstandings may occur between the two professionals is that of selection of children for therapy, as the criteria for referral used by teachers may not be the same as those used by therapists. Most often differences of opinion arise because teachers and therapists have a different understanding of the word 'language'. Consequently they have different approaches to their language work; to the children who have language difficulties, and to the possibilities for the subsequent remediation of language breakdown (Fleming *et al.* 1997).

Teacher training encourages language to be viewed in terms of oracy and literacy according to the requirements of the National Curriculum, so that teachers when assessing the children ensure that they have a general overview of their written and spoken skills. In practice, in terms of the children's communication skills, this means that teachers are usually aware of those children who have limited intelligibility, or those who do not express themselves fluently, and of course those who have difficulties with reading and spelling. Therapists, on the other hand, are trained to take a linguistically analytical approach to language. It is within their working remit to identify the linguistic level of breakdown of speech and language as well as to assess the implications and functional consequences of such difficulties. Thus, it is not surprising that certain children who may be considered to be 'very severe' by the teacher, may be analysed on the therapists' scale as 'not very severe' – and vice versa – and prioritisation of children who need to be seen by the therapist may become a contentious issue.

Teachers' perceptions of some children with communication problems may understandably be that 'they are lazy', or that 'they could do it if only they'd try', for it is only by such detailed assessment as a therapist is able to undertake that often subtle, though substantial underlying 'language specific' difficulties may be uncovered.

One of the compounding aspects of such differences of approach is that in many instances terminology which is seemingly the same will be used by each of the professionals to mean different things. For example, to the lay person the term 'pragmatics' relates to matters of practical significance, whereas to speech and language therapists it is a technical term referring to a specific aspect of interactional communication.

One of the other factors which may affect a teacher's prioritisation will be the behaviour exhibited by a child – which may often result from the child's frustrated attempts to communicate. Thus, in a large class, where the teacher is contending with children with many different types of problems, children with communication disorders may be prioritised differently by the teacher than by the therapist.

Obviously any differences of opinion will need to be clarified and compromises reached regarding which children are seen by the therapist. Adequate meeting and discussion time and mutually beneficial INSET, would also enable each to gain a better understanding of the other's standpoint (Shaw *et al.* 1996).

The effects of management

Who manages each of the professionals involved in a specific joint working relationship may have an important impact on the relationship itself. This may be with regard to the support received, expectations, or extramural commitments, all of which may exert additional pressures on the individuals concerned. Both the teachers and the therapists are members of their own professional teams, but the effects of such membership will vary according to the hierarchy of the management structure within each profession, the authority invested in the line manager, and the role the manager plays in relation to individual members of staff.

Rarely, unless they are both employed by the same agency, are they dually managed. Being independently managed will bring its own problems for it is not easy then to establish who has the ultimate authority, the power of decision-making and the ability to enable change to occur (Roberts 1994).

Most teachers are accountable to the Principal of their school. Head teachers are generally qualified teachers who work largely in an administrative role, having the authority to discipline and being involved in the 'hiring and firing'. At primary level, the head teacher is usually the line manager for all members of staff. At secondary level, a classroom teacher may be answerable initially to a head of department. Despite the possibilities of a shifting emphasis since LMS, the primary focus of all of the staff and management is the education of the child.

The hierarchy and management of therapists on the other hand is more varied, having undergone significant changes in recent years. This may serve to affect the focus of the therapists' work. Having initially been responsible to Senior Medical Officers or hospital administrators, after the 1974 reorganisation of the NHS, therapists for the first time were managed by members of their own profession. A hierarchical structure was imposed so that speech and language therapy managers became line managers with similar powers to head teachers. However, more recently, since the introduction of NHS Trusts, speech and language therapists may now be managed by a member of another therapy profession, or even by a business manager with no therapy training. This means that there is the possibility of a shift in the thrust and emphasis of therapists' work. This will affect the expected outcomes and the prioritisation of the workload in general and often the case-load in particular, which underlines the differences in expectations and achievement referred to above.

Geographical considerations

Not only are working relationships affected by the working conditions within a school, but also there are some external factors, such as where the schools are located, which may also have a significant effect on working conditions. For example, whether it is in an inner city area, rural area, urban or suburban area may affect the type of problems presented by the children, the availability of support services, and the ways in which those services are offered to the schools.

The children and their problems

In an inner city area, potentially there will be a much higher incidence of multicultural, multi-ethnic, multilingual children within the school system than in rural or urban districts and this will specifically impact upon the nature of the communication disorders found among the children. One of the primary considerations for the therapists will be to make the distinction between those children who are not developing speech and language normally because of an underlying communication disorder – a disorder which is also apparent in any language which may be used with the child at home; and those for whom delayed speech and language development is merely due to the fact that English is their second or third language. The latter group of children would be expected to catch up with their peers after a reasonable exposure to English, particularly once they have spent time in school. The former group are more likely to need specific help.

In terms of the management of communication disordered children from multilingual backgrounds, there are specific cultural issues which must be considered. For example, interpreters may be needed when assessing the children and gathering case history details, or when trying to discuss prognosis and management with the parents or carers. Additional factors must also be taken into account such as the fact that in different cultures there are different levels of acceptance of the existence of communication and learning difficulties, and different parental expectations with regard to the children's potential, particularly if the child is a firstborn son. According to the children's cultural/ethnic background, there will be differences in the parents' approach in general to impairment, disability and handicap, as well as in their attitude to 'the specialist' (see Chapter 2) and their willingness to be involved in any of the remedial work.

The effects of distance

Service provision

If the children live in a rural area then there are specific geographical implications which must be taken into account. For example, LEAs and HAs do not usually have the same boundaries, so that therapists employed by the NHS in one HA may be covering schools in more than one LEA, or one LEA may be served by more than one HA. According to the Manpower Planning Advisory Group survey (1991), the establishment of speech and language therapists in the UK is almost six whole time equivalent therapists per 100,000 population. With such a high ratio of potential clients per therapist, it can therefore be assumed that in less densely populated areas therapists will be expected to cover a large geographical area, and this will normally include a large number of schools which may be great distances apart. The amount of time spent travelling then becomes a serious consideration as it may affect the frequency as well as the length of the therapists' visits, and may result in the service being delivered in blocks of time with periods of no service, rather than a regular ongoing service.

Equally, if children have to visit the therapist in clinic, much time could be spent travelling to and fro, and the appropriateness of this will need to be carefully weighed against the positive effects of the therapy received. Such situations provide a strong basis for the argument for joint working practice; for, if the therapist can work with and through the teachers, the time wasted travelling (by either the therapists or the children) can be reduced, and the children can receive more regularly an extension of their therapy from the teacher or a classroom assistant within the school.

Service availability

Therapists in rural areas are often more isolated professionally, having to travel distances to meet up with colleagues in another part of the HA area. Potential contact with teachers will thus be equally problematic. Children living in urban or inner city areas often have more choice of services either through the NHS or the voluntary organisations. Specialist appointments, for example for audiological testing or to a Child Development Centre, may be easier to arrange, and tertiary referral for an expert speech and language therapy opinion may be more readily available and geographically closer for the child and carers to attend.

The effects of legislative changes

The Education Act (1981) – Statement of Special Educational Needs

Some of the recent legislation with specific regard to education has led to changes in patterns of support services provision which in some instances has had a direct effect on teacher/therapist working patterns. For example, there are some speech and language therapy services which are only in existence as a result of the 1981 Education (Handicapped Pupils) Act. This Act encouraged the LEAs to integrate children with special needs into mainstream education rather than segregating them into special schools or units. In some geographical areas this led to the development of a speech and language therapy service to mainstream schools where previously school-age children had been expected to attend the local clinic for therapy (Roux 1996), thus changing the whole pattern of service provision.

In some instances, speech and language therapy posts may have been created specifically to support the children with statements who had been integrated. The overall result of these new patterns of service delivery was an increase in the opportunities available for teachers and therapists to work together. This presented opportunities for therapists to reconceptualise their work in schools and in particular their work with teachers, although there was a need to grapple with some new specific issues, such as the prioritisation of children with statements as opposed to non-statemented children.

Statements of Special Educational Need which resulted directly from the Act may facilitate the working partnership of teachers and therapists in several different ways, in particular they encourage dyads to improve the ways in which they work together. For example, where a child already has a statement there can be no doubts or misunderstandings about the child's needs because they are clearly listed in the statement. Both professionals know that they are working towards a common goal and that they will each have to report individually on the child's progress in their specific area at the annual review.

The fact that a statement may be required for a child may also provide a common goal for a teacher and therapist as they may work together on their respective reports. The fact that they have both been instrumental in helping the child be statemented, and their subsequent involvement in its production, may in itself help to cement their working relationship.

It is possible that a teacher may have to liaise with more than one therapist. Different therapists may have been specifically contracted to work with each of the statemented children individually. Similarly, in a mainstream school which is in the private sector, because of the large catchment area covered by the school each of the children may be supported by one of several therapists each of whom could be visiting the school from different health authorities from far and wide!

Non-statemented children

There may be some instances where there are children in the same class with seemingly similar needs for whom a statement has not been produced. The Speech and Language Therapy Service still has a 'duty of care' to these non-statemented children and must offer equitable access to the service to all those with impaired communication. This duty, discharged by the therapists, is owed to all communication impaired children by the employing authority. They are beholden to provide assessment and diagnosis of the communication disorders, intervention, and decisions about the continuance of therapy for such children irrespective of whether the children have a Statement of Special Educational Needs (RCSLT 1997). It may be possible that non-statemented children may be covered by a different speech and language therapy services contract, which may result in different therapists visiting the same classroom. If one therapist visits the statemented children within a class and another supports the non-statemented children within the same class, naturally this may cause some difficulties – and even confusion – not only for the teacher who may have to work with more than one therapist, but also for the therapists. Needless to say close teacher–therapist working relationships in such situations may be difficult to develop and maintain.

Further and more far-reaching effects of integration and segregation will be further discussed in Chapters 5, 6, and 7.

The Education Reform Act (1988) – the National Curriculum

The second major piece of legislation to influence working relationships between the two professionals was the 1988 Education Reform Act through which the National Curriculum was introduced. As curriculum policy came into the public domain, for the first time therapists who were working with school-age children had access to the same curriculum documents as teachers. The wording used to outline the subjects and to explain the targets which children were expected to achieve in each of the subject areas gave teachers and therapists access to a shared terminology. This made it easier for therapy programmes to be planned which were more relevant to the children's classroom activities.

Within the English Curriculum, the development of oracy/spoken language was referred to explicitly and this was welcomed by both teachers and therapists. It was felt to be of particular importance in relation to younger children as they are assessed at the age of seven when it could be expected that the development of basic oral skills will be complete. The impact of the introduction of this aspect of the curriculum was such that, in some areas, therapists reported a rise in referral rates from schools as the teachers worked towards these attainment targets in the English Curriculum. However, as a result of these developments it also became apparent that children who were known to have had difficulties with speech and language prior to school entry were seen to be struggling when they were assessed at Key Stage 1. There is still some concern that children with communication problems may not always be able to achieve the attainment targets which seven year olds are expected to reach after only two years in primary school.

The Code of Practice (1994)

The Code of Practice on the Identification and Assessment of Special Educational Needs has also had a significant impact on individual teacher's working practice as well as speech and language therapy services, and consequently on teachers' and therapists' joint working practice. The recommendation in the Code that every school should have a SENCO means that within each school there should be a 'named' professional with whom the visiting speech and language therapist should automatically be able to liaise. This liaison could be with regard to general issues in relation to communication or about specific children. The SENCO will then be able to act as an intermediary, part of the triad of therapist, teacher and SENCO. The five-stage model which is outlined in the Code ensures that therapists should be included in the assessment of children with communication problems at least at stage 3, if not before. The evidence collected during stages 1 and 2 about the children's difficulties will provide a wealth of material for the teachers and therapists to consider alongside the therapists' assessments, thus encouraging a joint working approach.

Expectations and assumptions

In close working partnerships the effect of the perceptions, expectations and assumptions of each of the pair about the other must never be underestimated. The ways in which teachers and therapists perceive and view each others' professional role is of critical importance to the development of their working relationship for it will lead to certain expectations, some of which may be impossible to fulfil. Similarly, the expectations of the parents of the children must not be discounted. If there is a perceived mismatch between expectations and performance between either of the professionals, or between the professionals and the parents, then there is the danger that disgruntlement, resentment – and even anger – may begin to grow.

Unfortunately it is not uncommon for teachers and therapists to misunderstand each others' roles as there are many popular 'myths', misconceptions and misperceptions specifically about the role of the speech and language therapist. For example, being an employee of the NHS supports the 'medical' image of the therapist, feeding into the expectation that the therapy will provide a 'cure' for the children's 'problem' within a defined time period. Reid *et al.* (1996) even refer to 'the magic wand' phenomenon in this regard. As this is not the nature of the management of severe speech and language difficulties such an expectation can only lead to disappointment, and irritation when the effects of the therapy work are not always obviously apparent and 'changes' when they do occur may sometimes be over a long period of time.

Another 'myth' relates to the misinterpretation of the professional title 'speech and language therapist' and this too may contribute to others misunderstanding the therapists' role. Some teachers and parents fail to realise that the title encompasses all aspects of communication, including the acquisition and development of speech and the child's first language and the development of non-verbal communication skills such as body language, gesture and eye contact. As it is still not uncommon for therapists to be misidentified as elocution teachers or even as teachers of English as a second language, it is not surprising that teachers and parents do not always understand that therapists are also interested in children who do not have speech, and that they may be able to work with them on alternative and augmentative methods of communication.

In the same way, therapists often fail to understand the teachers' role in relation to the development of language within school, in particular in relation to oracy and literacy. Or, they may not understand the nature of the teachers' role with regard to managing and organising the other adults who may be working within the classroom – such as non-teaching assistants, nursery nurses, support teachers or even parent volunteers. This particularly may lead therapists to have unrealistic expectations about the amount of time teachers may be able to devote to an individual child in order to back up therapy, as they may not grasp fully the demands on the teacher within a busy classroom.

All of these seemingly harmless misconceptions can lead to a build up of resentment and frustration which will naturally impede the development of potential working harmony. Whichever obstacles apply to any specific dyad must be identified and overcome in order for smooth working patterns to develop into mutually beneficial joint working practices.

Chapter 5

Current practice in mainstream schools

Introduction

As highlighted in Chapter 4, as a result of educational legislation which has occurred since 1981, children with many different types of impairment and disability including primary or secondary communication difficulties are now able to take advantage of the option of *inclusive education*: they may be integrated into mainstream schools where they will be supported by services offered by a range of professionals, including speech and language therapists. In order to facilitate this integration and to enable the children to maximise their educational opportunities, all of the professionals involved, including the teachers, have had to reconsider their methods of approach when working with such children. In this chapter, implications of this inclusive education will be discussed, and some of the different approaches of teachers and speech and language therapists working together to support children who have been integrated into mainstream schools will be considered.

Inclusive education – integration into mainstream schools

One of the main benefits for children with special needs who are integrated into mainstream schools, and specifically for those with speech and language problems, is that the other pupils provide linguistic 'models' and, even more importantly, models of 'normal' social behaviour. The school provides a naturalistic environment for children in which communication skills are used in an almost prescribed way and where there are implicitly understood social rules. However, the size of a mainstream school will usually preclude the children from making large numbers of close relationships with children or staff. This is even more noticeable in a secondary setting where the schools are often large and even within one class pupils experience constant change. 'An understanding of the adjustments the child needs to make can help inform approaches to providing support' (Jacklin and Lacey 1993).

Educationally, the schools also provide common ground for the children for, within each mainstream school, whether it is a local state-run primary, secondary or comprehensive school; a grant maintained school; a religious school, or a private school, all children face the common demands of the National Curriculum. In addition, the expectations of the staff are that the children will learn not only from their lessons but also incidentally from their general life experiences within the educational and social context of their immediate environment. Thus, within the mainstream school setting, the performance of children with special educational needs is related to that of their peer group and they are competing with a larger number of pupils within the same age group than they would in a special school (Jacklin and Lacey 1993). While it may be necessary to make some modifications to the mode of delivery and/or the content of the curriculum for specific children such as those with multiple disabilities, children with special needs are not generally sheltered – as they might be in a segregated environment. Naturally, there will be some children with communication difficulties who will thrive in such a setting, although there will be others who will struggle, particularly those with additional complex needs.

However, it must be recognised that despite the advantages of the 'levelling' factor which is implicit in their acceptance into such schools, not all professionals within this system are adequately prepared for working inclusively with children with communication problems. For example, although the 1994 Code of Practice explicitly states that it is within the remit of all teachers in mainstream schools to take responsibility for any children with special needs within their class, many teachers do not have specific training in this area. Teachers generally are trained to work with children whose learning may be expected to develop steadily within the parameters of certain anticipated rates of progress – progress which is measured at prescribed intervals. These children are expected to transfer to a secondary school at the end of the primary phase of their education. Most teachers in a mainstream setting therefore will be ill-prepared for working with children whose progress may be delayed in relation to their peers.

Similarly, although speech and language therapists are trained to deal with children who have speech and language difficulties, and their slow rates of progress and improvement, they may not initially have experience of supporting children with such problems within a mainstream school setting. They will not necessarily understand the needs of the children in relation to the curriculum, or realise the specific strains which inclusive education may place on such children.

It becomes important, therefore, that teachers and therapists working with children with communication problems within this setting should develop good working relationships. They need to be able to pool their knowledge and experience in order to 'share the load' as they begin to find different approaches to their work with the children. In this way they may begin to understand the specific needs of the children and offer them the most appropriate and effective means of support. This will ensure that any advice given by the speech and language therapist will be directly related to the demands of the educational context and the curriculum (RCSLT 1997).

Working together – differences of approach

There can be no prescribed 'model' of working practice – there can only be a variety of models and methods which have been found to be beneficial. In the words of Jowett and Evans (1996): 'There is not a set way collaboration is tackled, so it is very much up to the individuals in that team'. The approaches taken, and the ways in which the professionals involved will respond to each other as well as to the educational needs of the children, will be influenced by many different factors. These include their initial training and any additional specialist training undertaken; their working experiences, and their previous experiences of joint working practice. In addition, there will be factors relating to the teachers, the therapists and the children specifically which will influence not only the approach of each of the individuals but also those within a dyadic working partnership.

The teachers' framework

According to the Code of Practice, each school's governing body has a statutory duty towards pupils with special educational needs, and within individual schools the teachers and non-teaching assistants will usually contribute towards the school-wide special educational needs policy. It is this policy which will govern the framework within which all the staff in that school will work with the children, and will help to establish the school ethos in respect of how staff relate to, and work with, visiting professionals. As discussed in Chapter 4, the structure of the school and the organisation of the individual classroom will constrain or encourage professional working relationships. The development of a partnership may be dependent on such factors as the number of assistants available to help the teacher, the number of children in the class and the administrative demands on the teacher's time.

The therapists' framework

Speech and language therapists also have a statutory duty to discharge the 'duty of care' as discussed above. The framework within which the therapists are able to relate to, and work with, teachers in mainstream schools will be influenced by several aspects of the overall speech and language therapy services such as:

- how the speech and language therapy service is offered;
- how that service is delivered by a specific speech and language therapy team;
- to whom the service is offered specifically as 'client'.

Offering the service

Some schools may employ their own therapists directly, but in most instances the service will be purchased from a local health authority, or community trust. The frequency with which the service is provided and the availability of the professionals will to some extent be determined by the geographical location of the school, the size of the area and the number of therapists available, as discussed in Chapter 4.

Delivery of the service

The ways in which a speech and language therapy service may be offered will also vary greatly, contingent upon many factors as outlined in Chapter 4. For example, a therapist may visit a school to work with individual children on a consistent and regular, though possibly infrequent, basis throughout the year; or one (or more than one) therapist may offer intensive therapy within a school for one term only each year (Roux 1996). Some therapists may provide INSET to the teaching staff so that initially they may be able to work *with* the teacher possibly with groups of children; with the long term aim that the therapy work will eventually be conducted *through* the teacher (Hoddell 1995) so that the frequency of visits by the therapist may be reduced. Such ways of working will be discussed in more detail below.

Who is the client?

In some instances it will be the individual children who are the clients. The therapist will focus on delivering therapy to the specific children within the contract, seeking support and follow-up within the school by liaising with the class teacher, the SENCO and any other support worker who may be providing non-teaching support for the children on a regular basis.

However, it is also possible that a therapist may provide a speech and language therapy service to a school, so that it is 'the school' who is the 'client'. The therapist will then be contracted to work with any children within that school who require help. The pattern of visits to such schools will vary according to the therapist's workload. For example, some therapists may visit all the schools for which they are responsible once a term. The teachers, or SENCO, may then provide a list of children who are causing concern regarding communication skills for the therapists to screen and assess.

The influence of the children's communication problems

The ways in which individual children may be most successfully supported and maintained by teachers and therapists in a mainstream class will of course vary according to the nature of the specific problem. This will be dependent upon whether communication is the primary problem or is a secondary problem resulting from the presence of more complex difficulties. For example, a different approach will be needed for a child whose primary problem is a severe language impairment associated with specific learning difficulties (dyslexia), from that used with a child whose communication problems are the result of a cognitive deficit such as in children with Down's syndrome. A different method of approach again may be needed for a child whose communication problem is a secondary feature of a physical disability such as cerebral palsy. However, the approach taken by the professionals will also be dependent upon:

- whether or not the communication problems were identified prior to school entry;
- once identified, whether or not their needs have been written into a statement.

The implications of these different factors need to be considered carefully.

Working with children whose communication problems have not been identified prior to school entry

Late identification

A communication problem is often identified – and dealt with – prior to school entry, as discussed in Chapter 4. However, there may be several reasons why such problems may not become apparent until the children begin to attend school full time.

This may be because, within the familiar home environment, communication patterns become set and predictable; the context and basic vocabulary used is common to all so that the children's speech is understood by those within the immediate circle of family and friends. The children may not often talk to strangers outside of that circle, and may not have been placed in unfamiliar situations. In other cases, children's developmental speech and language problems may remain undetected if there are no siblings and no young children within the immediate social environment with whom parents may compare their child.

Often, children develop coping strategies which mask their problems so that, even where some difficulties are recognised, they may not appear to be severe enough to warrant intervention. Once children enter school, however, it usually becomes more difficult for them to continue to disguise such problems. Their previously adequate coping strategies may begin to break down, exposing and highlighting their communication difficulties. Classroom based activities place a different level of demands on children. They are required to interact with many different, unfamiliar children and adults – possibly for the first time – in situations where the context of their speech is not necessarily known and the vocabulary not anticipated, so that they may not automatically be understood. Thus, in school, activities such as speaking out in front of the whole class during 'circle time' or 'show and tell' may become important first indicators of children's communication difficulties.

Similarly, it may be impossible for children to continue to disguise pre-existing problems when work begins on literacy skills within the classroom. Then, children who may have minimal difficulties with the production of some speech sounds – or children whose pre-school therapy has enabled them to successfully overcome an earlier speech problem – may display specific difficulties when learning to read and spell. This often indicates that there is an underlying deficit which has affected all aspects of their developing language skills (Stackhouse 1996) and their literacy difficulties will need to be specifically addressed.

Recognising the problems

If speech and language problems are not manifest until after school entry, then the classroom teachers may play a key role in identifying the children who appear to be experiencing difficulties. Teachers are in a prime position to observe children within the enclosed and familiar school environment so that they not only have the knowledge about the children's abilities in the classroom and the ways in which they adapt to the classroom routine, but also about how they behave and mix with their peers. In addition, teachers have useful information about children's patterns of attendance and general health, other factors which usually prompt them to recognise readily the children who appear to be struggling (Fleming *et al.* 1997).

Indeed, speech and language therapists rely on the school staff to bring such children to their attention. In accordance with their professional standards and guidelines (RCSLT 1996), which stipulate that it is part of a speech and language therapist's remit to help school staff by providing appropriate INSET, some therapists have developed training packages specifically to aid this process and to enable teachers to make more accurate referrals to speech and language therapy services (Shaw *et al.* 1996). Teachers and therapists are then in a position to pool important knowledge and information about the children. They can put together the results of the therapists' more formal assessments with the teachers' informal observations in order to confirm the children's areas of difficulty.

Identifying the children with more obvious problems

Most teachers are readily able to recognise children who have overt communication difficulties – for example, those who respond in a significantly different manner to activities within the classroom; children who have difficulties interacting and communicating with their peers; children who are willing to join in expressive, verbal activities but whose speech is not clearly intelligible; or children who obviously avoid speaking out in class, trying not to answer questions or read aloud because when they do attempt to speak their speech is disfluent (that is, they 'stammer'). Teachers are normally in a position to refer children with any of these problems directly to the speech and language therapist.

Identifying the children with less obvious problems

There are many instances, however, when the children's problems may be more covert, and it may not be obviously apparent that the behaviours displayed by specific children are in fact the manifestation or the result of communication difficulties. The behaviours may be interpreted in many different ways and may not lead a teacher to register an 'expression of a concern' (Code of Practice 1994, para 2:71) in relation to the children's communication skills. It is important that communication difficulties are considered, however, whenever children display such behaviours, as failure to recognise the possible cause may delay the provision of appropriate help. Some of these behaviours are described below.

Behaviours related to attention (or possibly to comprehension) difficulties

- The children may have difficulty in attending to instructions and the lesson content.

- They may constantly move around the room – playing with objects, interacting with and distracting other children, not concentrating on the activity or primary task of the lesson. This may be due to poor attention skills, or may indicate that the children are having difficulties comprehending the task.
- They may constantly seek the attention of the teacher and/or any other adults in the classroom.

Behaviours related to comprehension difficulties

- The children may appear slow to follow instructions. They may be the last ones to complete a task, or they may fail to carry out a complete set of instructions.
- The children may constantly copy or watch other children before beginning a task because they have not understood the instructions.
- They may appear talkative but much of what they say may be lacking in content. They merely echo what others say to them because they do not fully understand the spoken word.

Behaviours related to cognitive difficulties

- These children may be slow to learn the class routine; have problems with concepts of time and space; have difficulties with general organisational skills. An inability to understand the basic concepts means that they will then not understand, or be able to use, the appropriate vocabulary related to such concepts and may not, for example, be able to sequence their ideas or their actions.
- There may be some children who have difficulties telling a story in sequence; they may appear not to have the requisite vocabulary, or have difficulty setting the story into a time frame.

Behaviours related to social, interactional and pragmatic communication skills

- These children may be seen to be socially inept, or gauche, and may seem to be socially isolated, appearing to be 'loners' in the crowd, not associating with others. This may be because their play skills are inappropriate so that they are unable to play with – or even alongside – other children; or it may be that they lack the linguistic skills needed to approach others and initiate conversations.

- In class, these children may appear withdrawn; lacking in confidence, unable to initiate conversations, answer questions, or to contribute to group discussions.
- Some children do not appear to understand the different language codes used in different settings so that their own verbal responses may be inappropriate. Often this results in them being told off for 'being silly'.
- There are some children who take the meanings of all words literally. They do not appreciate sarcasm or understand when words are used in idiomatic expressions. For example, 'cut that out' meaning 'stop it' might induce such children to search for scissors or a means of literally 'cutting out' some unspecified 'thing'.

Behaviours relating to expressive language

- There may be children who appear eager to answer questions in class, but who have nothing to say when they are asked a question directly, because they have difficulties accessing the words voluntarily. If they do respond they may have a limited vocabulary compared with the other children.
- Some children's difficulties are even more specific for they cannot recall even the most commonly used, newly learned vocabulary. It is easy to attribute such problems to forgetfulness or laziness, whereas in fact this may be indicative of a serious linguistic deficit.
- Similarly it is easy to dismiss children who seem to be able to 'read' the printed word but who cannot answer questions about what they have just read. This may mean that they have a serious problem with understanding the written word, even if they are able to decode it.

Procedure for the teachers

If teachers identify children with communication difficulties, it is their responsibility to ensure that appropriate action is subsequently taken. They may liaise with the SENCO within the school and discuss their concerns with the children's parents, possibly seeking parental permission for the children to be referred to a speech and language therapist. This may be done as an informal procedure or more formally as part of stage 3 of the Code of Practice. However, if as in some schools the speech and language therapist is providing the school with a consultation service, it may be possible for permission to be sought for the children to be referred earlier.

Working together – the initial meeting

Once the children have been identified and referred for speech and language therapy it is important that the teacher and therapist set up an initial meeting as quickly as possible so that they may decide on their working strategies. If the two professionals are to work together successfully, this initial meeting is crucial as it will set a blueprint for the future pattern of their developing working relationship. Once they both accept joint responsibility for the children's communication problem, then they will be able to establish a division of labour so that the teacher may be involved in the therapy programme in a practical and manageable way.

At this meeting, therefore, they will need to discuss what each is able to offer in terms of knowledge, skills and time commitment, so that there can be no misunderstanding regarding what each may expect the other to provide. It can be disappointing and will be counter-productive if there is a mismatch of expectations (see Chapter 3). Having reached an understanding regarding each other's contribution, it is also important that they both have realistic expectations of the possible outcome of any therapy work undertaken, so that there are no false assumptions about therapy effecting an automatic 'cure' for the children's communication problems.

If they are able to establish at the initial meeting that it is not only the children who would benefit from input from both of them, but also that they as professionals can gain from each other, then they should be able to agree to pool their knowledge from the outset in order to save duplication of effort. Thus, even at the first meeting they may be able to share information about previous contact with the child and possibly with the child's parents which they may have had. The teacher will already have had the opportunity to make important observations regarding the child's speech and language problems: how they are manifest in the classroom; the impact they are having on the child's learning, and any successful, or unsuccessful, teaching strategies which may already have been tried.

Agreement will need to be reached about the ways in which the therapist may undertake further assessment and how the results of these findings will contribute to a holistic picture of the child's overall needs. Between them the two professionals may then decide how therapy may best be undertaken given the constraints of the school, in general and the classroom specifically, and how specific adaptations may be made to suit the needs of individual children. Thus, for example they may agree which children would benefit from being withdrawn individually by the therapist; which children might be considered for group work within the classroom, and how any follow-up work may be undertaken by the teacher or non-teaching assistant. This will be discussed in more detail below in relation to children whose problems have already been identified.

Working with children whose communication problems have been identified prior to school entry

As discussed in Chapter 4, children with communication problems may have been working with a speech and language therapist from an early age, before they attend school or even nursery. It is helpful therefore if, at the beginning of a new term, the therapist is able to identify for the SENCO or head teacher of a primary school, as appropriate, any children of those newly admitted to the school who have previously attended the speech and language therapy clinic. These children will fall into two basic categories:

- those whose communication problems have been recorded on a statement of special educational needs;
- those who do not have a statement of special educational needs.

Children who have communication problems which are recorded on a statement of special educational needs

For many children their communication problems are identified before they enter school and their class teachers will be aware of their problems, for they will be recorded as part of each child's statement of special educational needs. The information written into the statement should include details regarding the child's needs in relation to speech and language therapy support that the child should receive. In many cases children's parents will already have discussed details of therapy provision with the head teacher before their children begin to attend the school. Some children may have already received speech and language therapy in their pre-school years and their parents may try to ensure that this at least continues or, if possible, increases. Indeed, often they may agree to a statement being written for their child with the expectation that therapy may then be provided within the school.

Children who have communication problems but do not have a statement of special educational needs

There are several reasons why a child with a communication problem may not have a statement of special educational needs. It may be because it is felt that the type of communication problem does not warrant a statement, or because local policy or school policy does not encourage statements to be written for such children. It is possible, however, that children's behaviour once they start attending school, and their difficulties with coping either educationally and/or socially in school, influences the head teacher or the therapist so that a request may be made for a statement to be considered. For, although a statement will not guarantee the automatic provision of service, it will identify the children's requirements and needs, and it will protect the provision and services

However, as discussed above, irrespective of whether children with communications problems have a statement, therapists are bound by a 'duty of care' to provide a speech and language therapy service. In fact, in some areas such children form the majority of the speech and language therapists' case-load. Often they may be seen with the same frequency and regularity as children who have a statement, but this may not always be the case.

Laying the foundations for mutual support

At the initial meeting between teachers and therapists concerned with children whose problems have already been identified, many of the same issues will need to be discussed as outlined above regarding children whose problems have not yet been identified. However, there will be two important differences. Firstly, it may be possible for the meeting to take place very early in the term, before the children have settled in, in order to anticipate any potential problems which may result within the classroom. Secondly, as the initial assessment has already taken place, discussion will need to focus on the ways in which the communication problems may be manifest in the classroom and how these may impact on the children's learning (Daines *et al.* 1996).

Practical matters must be dealt with as quickly as possible so that the teacher and therapist will need to establish where the therapist will be situated and how the therapy will be offered. They will need to agree which children should be withdrawn from the class, and which will be seen individually. The teacher and therapist need to identify what they feel are their areas of concern, in terms of their working together as well as in relation to specific children.

They will then need to share their aims and objectives, as the partnership may be enhanced if they have common goals. These meetings in the early stages of the partnership will also provide opportunities for discussion about the nature of the therapy which the therapist will provide and the teaching strategies which the teacher may wish to employ in order to support the therapy. This is particularly relevant to the development of the professionals' relationship because it has been suggested that when both the teachers and the therapists are involved with the planning of therapy in this way they feel a greater sense of ownership and commitment to their work with the child (Wright 1992).

Decisions need to be made regarding meeting times so that there is careful planning and organisation regarding how, when and where they intend to share information. If the therapist visits the school only occasionally, discussions between the teacher and therapist will usually be brief, so that conciseness and specific focus will be the essence of their meetings. If the therapists' visits to a school are on a regular basis they may be invited to join additional meetings, for example with educational psychologists and other members of staff.

This highlights the fact that work such as this between teachers and therapists may have resource implications beyond the classroom; beyond the two professionals concerned. For when children with communication problems are admitted into mainstream schools, the implications affect the school as a whole. Of course the ways in which the support for any children is delivered is influenced by the school policy relating to the support of statemented children. Naturally it is helpful if the school policy encourages management support for the teaching and support staff, and recognises the need for interprofessional meetings and discussion.

At the initial meeting, the teacher and therapist also need to identify other staff within the school generally and within the classroom specifically with whom information about the children needs to be shared. This may include the SENCO, subject teachers, any visiting learning support teachers, or non-teaching/learning support assistants who may work within the school. Naturally this will have further implications for the use of the school resources and time allocation, but it is important for the teacher and therapist to be able to plan realistically how the therapy may be followed up in the absence of the therapist. In addition, if the therapist is working in the classroom, it is also important to establish the roles of other adults who may work in the classroom – for example, regarding discipline in relation to the children and, more generally, in respect of the lines of management.

By the end of the initial stages both professionals should have laid the foundations for their future working patterns, and have realistic expectations regarding the level of involvement and support each is able to provide for the child – as well as for each other.

Ways of working together

It may be helpful in some situations if the teachers are able to observe some of the therapist's sessions, to see first hand the therapist's specific approach to the children's difficulties. In other cases it may be possible for the therapist to work innovatively within a specific school, not just recreating the intervention offered in the clinic. Thus for example, in a primary school the teacher and therapist may be able to share the space in the classroom. This may be done in a variety of ways. Each may work independently in different parts of the classroom, or they may decide to work together on a theme or activity but with specific groups of children. If there are other adults in the classroom, they too may be utilised in such a way as to make use of small group settings. In this way the children with the communication problems may be involved simultaneously in activities with the rest of their class, with a designated adult being responsible for ensuring that the activities are appropriately focused.

The teachers and therapists may be able to prepare joint worksheets for the children so that it is possible to bring together aspects of therapy and study skills within the classroom. Where children have IEPs, it is helpful if therapists are able to attend the meetings where these are discussed and planned. Then it should be possible to incorporate the children's communication needs with their academic needs. If the therapists are not able to attend such meetings, it is helpful if therapy goals can be presented on their behalf by the teachers so that they may be integrated appropriately into the plans. This may be particularly relevant in ensuring that significant links are forged between the development of the children's speech, and their language and literacy skills. Such combined goal setting and planning not only provides opportunities for the continuity of therapy, but also ensures that the therapy is relevant and appropriate for the children in relation to their academic work.

If a non-teaching assistant or helper has been assigned to work with specific children then this may work in one of two ways. It may be that the therapist works with the teacher who then closely works with and supervises the non-teaching assistant; or the therapist may arrange to meet with the non-teaching assistant on a more regular basis in order to supervise the work more directly. It is often more appropriate for therapists to suggest the therapy activities based on their assessment findings while others who are in more regular contact with the children will carry out the frequently required therapy (Reid *et al.* 1996). In order to support this method of working, some specific teaching materials have been produced by speech and language therapists such as Geliot (1993); Hall (1990) and Cooke and Williams (1985).

When working in this way it is important to establish the areas of responsibility and an agreed method for communication between the therapist, teacher and the non-teaching assistant and/or the SENCO so that the lines of authority are clearly assigned and understood. Frequent meetings will need to be held by some combination of the team to ensure:

- that the instructions which have been given are clear, unambiguous and workable;
- that they are understood in relation to the aims and objectives for the specific children;

- that the work is being carried out satisfactorily;
- that a concise but accurate record is kept of activities undertaken;
- that the work is evaluated so that records can be kept of progress made.

Where possible, follow-up discussions should succeed the therapy sessions as closely as possible as this will be the most constructive and useful way of ensuring continuity. However, it must be recognised that this is not always possible to achieve.

It is always important for therapists to keep comprehensive and contemporaneous records regarding their own work with the children (RCSLT 1997) and to keep copies in the school files of their records so that the teachers have easy access to them at any time. It may also be useful for teachers and therapists to compare notes regarding the children's behaviour, to determine whether it differs when they are with the therapist from how they behave in class.

However, it may also be possible for teachers and therapists to share aspects of their record keeping. Firstly, as discussed above, it is helpful if they can jointly record their aims for the term. In this way they can ensure that the educational aims and the therapy aims are realistic and workable for each individual child. Secondly, if they can find a way of combining the teacher's educational recording and the notes which the therapist needs to record regarding the progress of the children, then they may be able to reduce the amount of time needed at the end of the year when they will be required to gather such information for any of the children who may have an annual review. If they are able to review the progress of the children on a termly basis this will not only enable frequent evaluation and contribute to planning for future intervention, but may also be another way of accumulatively acquiring relevant material for any annual report.

Apart from work which may be undertaken together directly in relation to therapy for specific children, some teachers and therapists have also found it helpful to utilise each other's knowledge and skills in order to enhance their own professional development, so that they share articles, books and journals across the disciplines.

One of the specific areas in which a therapist can offer help which indirectly relates to the children is with regard to the teachers' input. When a child is identified as having difficulties with language in the classroom then the teachers need to reflect on their own language. They need to consider whether or not they need to modify the complexity of their utterances, the level of abstraction and the speed of their speech in order to help those children with communication difficulties. It may be that the language used by all adults in the classroom needs to be considered to ensure that children with communication problems will not be disadvantaged, for example by complex or abstract instructions (Daines *et al.* 1996).

Working apart but maintaining contact

Of course, there are situations where it is not possible for the therapist to work with the children within the school, and consequently the liaison with the teacher will be of a different nature. If the children visit the therapist at the health centre, it may be possible for the therapist to make a specific visit to the school in order to meet with the teacher for discussion. Sometimes visits are only possible at irregular intervals as it may prove difficult to arrange a mutually convenient time. Alternatively, arrangements may be made for therapists to assess the children, and for them to send to the school planned programmes to support therapy so that the teachers may follow through within the classroom. This may be important if contact cannot be maintained in any other way for, according to the professional standards and guidelines (RCSLT 1996), therapists are expected to provide a written programme outlining areas of difficulty for the children and offering details regarding appropriate intervention.

Maintaining contact with parents

When a speech and language therapy service is delivered to children directly within a school there is a risk of therapists losing contact with the parents. Most therapists have close links with the children and their families prior to school entry, particularly with the parent who brings the children to the health centre, but this diminishes once the children start school. The teachers naturally often have frequent contact with the parents, particularly if parents have specific concerns about their children and it may be to the teachers that parents will express their frustration if they are no longer able to contact the therapist directly.

Jowett and Evans (1996) found that parents were reassured by regular contact with therapists who worked with their children's schools, so it is important for therapists to ensure that if they are no longer seeing the children in the health centre they either make home visits, keep in telephone contact with parents or contact parents indirectly through the teachers. Contact on a weekly basis enabled Almond (1997) to work with her son in a realistic way without being overwhelmed by the enormity of the overall problem. She felt that such regular contact 'gave her back her freedom to work with him'. Keeping such connections may be another important way in which teachers and therapists may share the load.

Chapter 6

Current practice in special schools

Introduction

Although there are many advantages to inclusive education, as discussed in Chapter 5, there is still a place in the educational system for special school provision for children with specific types of problems. This is often most appropriate for children with more complex needs who may benefit from a setting which is 'relatively small, intimate and hopefully well staffed' (Wrynne 1986), where consistent and constant specialist help can be offered from a range of services, providing a supportive environment. Special schools are usually relatively small and all the children and staff are usually known to each other and have a characteristically close relationship (Jacklin and Lacey 1993).

Special schools offer places to children with a wide range of disabilities. The academic approach of each individual school and the educational and therapy support which may be available will vary according to the type of children, the severity of their problems and the complexity of their needs, as well as the resources which are available to meet those needs.

Within special schools there may often be adaptations and modifications to the fabric of the building itself. This may include the classrooms so that the school may become a pleasanter, safer and more user-friendly place for children who, for example, may have difficulties with mobility, or have a visual impairment; or for those who are profoundly deaf.

However, more importantly, special schools provide a setting in which the National Curriculum can be modified in order to accommodate the needs of a cross section of children with similar problems, and where support services may be concentrated and integrated so that children's education and therapy may become closely woven and interlinked. In most special schools there is a large staff to pupil ratio, the composition of the class is constant and, generally, appropriate support staff work closely alongside the teachers. This of course has implications for teachers and therapists working together for, usually, there are many more opportunities for close working relationships to develop between staff working in special schools than there are for professionals working in mainstream schools.

A historical perspective

In the past, it was the responsibility of the LEAs to provide special education in separate, segregated schools for most of the children who fell into the 11 categories defined by the 1945 Handicapped Pupils and School Health Services Regulations (see Chapter 1). After 1974, this included schools for children with learning disabilities. However, the changes in approach which resulted in, and followed on from the educational legislation of the 1980s (see Chapter 1) has meant that there have been significant changes in the educational provision offered by some LEAs.

The 1994 Code of Practice, in particular, underlined the fact that children with special educational needs require a continuum of provision. This includes special units and special schools covering many different disabilities; for there remains a need for some segregated, specialist provision, particularly for children whose needs are so complex and severe that they cannot be met within the mainstream educational system. Many of these children will have associated communication disorders which will be catered for within the schools' special facilities. Special schools for children whose primary problems are related to communication, specifically spoken and written speech and language problems, have also been available since the late 1940s and continue to flourish. Currently, children with speech and language problems may be found in a variety of different types of special schools.

Funding issues

Special schools may be administered by the LEA or may be funded by charitable organisations such as the Autistic Society, SCOPE, the Royal

National Institute for the Blind, or voluntary sector charitable organisations which cater more specifically for speech and language problems such as I CAN. The type of educational provision offered by such schools may vary, often being influenced by the geographical situation of the school as well as by the funding which is available. It must be recognised that not all boroughs for example, are necessarily able to support such developments in their area. In the case of day schools this may be because there are not sufficient numbers of children requiring such a school living within the catchment area, so that children may have to go outside of their own local authority to find the specialist facility they require. Some LEAs may be unwilling to fund a school which will be attended mainly by children from outside the borough – children who will be bussed in each day.

From the parents' point of view, if they wish their children to attend special schools and there is no local provision, they then have to consider whether the borough in which they live may be willing to fund their children to attend special schools outside of their own catchment areas. Where such facilities are not available, parents may decide to send their children to residential schools rather than to local mainstream schools if that is the only alternative. One facility which has been developed in many boroughs in response to this difficulty is the specialist unit, a move which has been supported by professionals and parents. However, this does not always provide the solution as there are usually a limited number of places within each individual unit, and units are not always able to meet the needs of all the children requiring specialist help within the area. Special units will be discussed in more detail in Chapter 7.

Special schools

Irrespective of whether they are funded by a specific charity or by the LEA, special schools cater for children with a range of different problems. In relation to children with communication difficulties, these may be categorised according to whether the children's speech and language difficulties are a secondary problem or whether the school caters specifically for children whose primary problem is a speech and language disorder. In both instances, there are some schools in which, because of their location, most children are required to board; and others which may only be attended on a daily basis.

Residential schools

For many years, residential schools were the only option for children who had severe sensory, physical or speech and language problems if their parents required them to receive specialist teaching and therapy in the same venue. Although parents may now have other options, there are still advantages for some children in attending such schools. For example, in residential schools children are able to develop their academic and social skills consistently alongside other children who share the same problems. It is accepted that it may be more difficult for some parents to maintain frequent contact with staff if their children attend residential schools than if they attended day schools. Nevertheless, it is possible for strong links to be forged between most parents and the teachers, therapists and care staff. Thus for many children a residential setting remains a viable option.

Day schools

For many parents, however, day schools which offer specialist provision are a far more attractive alternative to their residential counterparts. Such schools normally offer all the advantages of residential schools: small classes; specialist teachers; and closely linked support staff. However, they naturally have the additional bonus that the children are able to live at home, and remain in daily contact with their family support system. It is often easier for parent–staff links to develop more closely than links between staff and parents of special needs children attending regular mainstream schools, and parents will often be specific about what they expect from the staff and the multidisciplinary team working together in relation to their children.

However, as referred to above, special day schools covering each type of disability are not located in every area. The appropriate special school will not necessarily be the 'local' school for all the children needing such provision. Although this may be satisfactorily resolved if financial agreement is reached between the boroughs involved, it may be necessary for some children to travel long distances – often one, or even two hours on the special school bus – at the beginning and end of each day in order to be able to attend an appropriate school. This could be a serious disadvantage for the children. Not only does the teaching day become significantly shorter than in equivalent local mainstream schools, but the length of time the children are away from home each day becomes considerably longer.

Schools for children whose impaired communication is a secondary problem

Some schools specialise in working with children's primary cognitive, sensory, physical or emotional problems. However, although the school may 'specialise', the populations are rarely homogeneous as the children who attend such schools will have a range of difficulties, many having extremely complex needs. Indeed, for some children with severe problems it may be difficult to identify the area of their greatest need when choosing the appropriate category of school for them to attend. Most of these children will also have communication difficulties and these will normally be addressed as part of the school curriculum. However, although speech and language therapy will usually be provided, communication will probably not be the primary thrust of the schools' programmes.

Schools for children whose impaired communication is a primary problem

This will not be the case in schools which specialise in working with children whose primary problems are their speech and language disorders for, in such schools, communication will normally be the major area of concern. Although it must be recognised that some of the children who attend such schools may also have additional areas of difficulty which need to be accommodated, the primary focus in these special schools throughout the working day will be on the development of speech, language and communication skills. Naturally, the resourcing of speech and language therapy services in this type of school will differ from that which is available for schools for physically disabled children or children with emotional and behavioural difficulties, as a greater input from speech and language therapists will be required.

Schools for different age groups

Unlike the mainstream school system, there are not always separate special schools for primary-aged and secondary-aged children. In many cases, the secondary-age group are catered for on the same site and within the same facility as the primary-aged children, though usually they will have separate classes. The level of speech and language therapy provision, therefore, and the opportunities for teachers and therapists to work together, will vary according to the schools' resources but will not differ substantially because of the different ages of the children.

Support services for children with communication problems

The ways in which the education and additional support services are provided within special schools for children with speech and language problems will depend primarily upon whether the children have a primary or secondary communication problem. This will affect not only the ways in which the school day is organised, but also the range of staff who are employed to work within the school, and the ways in which those staff work with the children – and with each other. In residential schools all the staff are usually employed by the same authority or organisation, even though the terms and conditions of their contracts may differ according to the individual staff member's profession. This may also be the case in some day schools, particularly those funded by charitable organisations.

Irrespective of whether the therapist is a school employee, in special schools support services such as speech and language therapy are usually available within the school, and the ratio of children to therapists within any special school will normally be lower than in mainstream schools. Even where special assessment and consultation services may be available outside of the school, for example at a Child Development Centre for children with more complex needs, children would not be expected to attend regular therapy sessions at a health centre. Thus speech and language therapists will be found in most special schools which cater for a range of special educational needs such as cerebral palsy or severe learning difficulties, as well as those catering primarily for children with specific speech and language problems (Haynes and Naidoo 1991), although the distribution in terms of service delivery may be different.

Although there will normally be some level of speech and language therapy provision in schools where communication is a secondary problem for the children, there will rarely be more than one therapist working within the school. As in the mainstream system, if therapists are not solely assigned to a school or employed by a school, they will not necessarily be able to spend more time within an individual special school than in a specific mainstream school. They may be similarly assigned to work in more than one school, or to spend their time performing other duties.

Not surprisingly, in schools which cater primarily for children with specific speech and language problems, there is usually more than one speech and language therapist available within the school as there will be a greater emphasis on speech and language work within the framework of the curriculum. The therapists may even be employed by the school. This naturally will have implications for the development of teacher–therapist working relationships as therapists may be assigned to particular classes and work mainly with individual teachers.

This increased ratio not only of therapists to teachers but also of therapists to children will naturally increase the opportunities for the teachers and therapists to work together and will have implications for the way in which the two professionals are able to develop a working relationship. For as Reid *et al.* (1996) found as a result of their research in Scotland: 'where the ratio of [speech and language therapists] SLT to pupils, and also the ratio of SLT to education staff, is very high . . . the levels of all types of collaboration between SLTs and other staff are correspondingly high'. Such staffing levels hopefully encourage the development of a close rapport between the therapists and the children and also between all members of the staff, enabling them to work closely together in a naturalistic and practical way.

The development of a specialism

In order to work more successfully with children with physical, sensory, cognitive or emotional difficulties, who incidentally have communication difficulties, speech and language therapists often endeavour to develop a specialism in the primary area of concern. Thus, some speech and language therapists may specialise in working with deaf people, or with people with severe learning disabilities, learning to manage the children's communication difficulties which occur as a result of the primary disabilities, specifically within the context of their primary problems. However, this means that such therapists are then restricted to working in special schools which cover their area of specialisation: for example, therapists specialising in working with children with moderate or severe learning disabilities would not be able to work at the same level of competence with deaf children.

Sometimes, specialist therapists are employed to work in one specific special school. More frequently such therapists are used as a resource across an HA or LEA, covering all the schools within a given area which relate to their specialism. There are some specialist therapists for whom visits to special schools are only a part of their job. They may, in addition, run specialist clinics; support specific children in mainstream schools; run INSET courses, and deal with tertiary referrals advising other therapists within their district, and even from other areas.

Some therapists may develop specialist skills which are relevant across a range of different client groups. For example, they may develop a specialism in relation to all the different types of AAC systems which may be used with any communication impaired children. Or they may become specialists in feeding and swallowing problems (dysphagia) in children. They are then in a position to offer their expertise to a range of schools where they will be able to share their specialist knowledge with teachers who have their own special skills and knowledge to offer in return, as Kersner and Wright (1996) found in schools for children with severe learning disabilities.

Therapists working in special schools for speech and language disordered children will usually develop specialist skills in the assessment and treatment of Specific Language Impairment, and associated Specific Learning Difficulties. They may also specialise in the use of specific AAC systems which may be employed by the school for the more severely affected children.

Although it is not a prerequisite for working in a special school, teachers often have specialist qualifications either in the general area of special needs or in relation to specific disabilities. Usually they work in a specific type of special school because they have chosen to do so and often the majority of teachers within a special school will have many years of experience working with children with special needs.

The development of joint working practice

Thus it can be seen that although there may be some therapists who are attached exclusively to one special school – and even some schools with more than one therapist – this is not always the case. There are a large number of different types of schools which need to be covered by a limited number of therapists; a situation which is similar to that in mainstream provision. Although many LEAs have, over the years, negotiated with health authorities in order to improve this situation, there are still many schools where therapy provision is limited. Infrequent visits, and limited time spent by therapists in schools means that often teachers in special schools will encounter many of the same difficulties as teachers in mainstream schools when trying to work closely with therapists. In fact, despite the improved staff to pupil ratios, the problems may be compounded by the large numbers of children within each of the special schools who, by the nature of their primary difficulties, will need some degree of specialist help to enable the development of their communication skills.

Aspects which encourage joint working practice

There are however many specific features of special schools which encourage and enable joint working practice between teachers and therapists. Primarily there is the fact that all the children have special educational needs, so that all of the staff members are primed for managing the children's specific problems. The staff recognise that the children have problems learning and that their rates of progress may be slower than children in mainstream schools so that together they work towards the major goals: to educate the children; to help them realise their potential; and to enable the children, as far as possible, to live full and independent lives.

In some special schools, as part of their policy, specific commercial published programmes may be adopted, such as speech and language programmes, which are then implemented across the whole school. This often encourages staff to work together as they all become involved in some aspect of the programme. Thus for example, teachers and therapists are provided with a 'common language', a common focus in relation to the children, a specific context within which to communicate. Staff interaction is required not only in order to achieve their common goals for the children in relation to the programme, but to discuss aspects of its implementation. It may be necessary for the speech and language therapists, or for specialist teachers, to offer INSET to the remaining staff to help them understand such programmes and to train them to use them. This may apply for example to speech and language programmes such as the Derbyshire Language Scheme (Knowles and Masidlover 1982) which may be introduced into several different classes at the same time so that the children may work at appropriately increasing levels as they progress through the school.

Similarly, in schools where many children may need to use an AAC system to support spoken English, school policy may determine that specific systems are implemented school wide. It will be the role of the speech and language therapist or specialist teacher to introduce the system into the school, and to train staff with regard to its implementation, once again offering a specific focus to the encouragement of continued staff interaction. Having a school-wide alternative communication system will be of benefit to all the children who are struggling to communicate, as it will help to reduce confusion and frustration. It will mean that there is an automatic increase in the community with whom they are able to communicate, for everyone within the school will be using the same system. For example, in a school for children with specific speech and language impairment which has adopted Paget Gorman Signed Speech (PGSS) as its primary manual AAC system, children will automatically be able to communicate at some level, using PGSS, with all staff members as well as with most of the pupils throughout the school, as soon as they begin to learn some basic signs. It will also encourage communication among the staff, as they learn to implement the medium school wide.

Within special schools not only are there usually smaller classes, and improved staff to pupil ratios, but there is also a greater adult to pupil ratio within each class, than is generally found in mainstream schools. For, in addition to the teachers, therapists and classroom assistants, there may be helpers – parents, volunteers or students – in many special school classrooms. Many schools also have a wide range of professionals who work with the children in the school, so that in any classroom there may be a combination of physiotherapists, occupational therapists, nurses, specialist teachers and psychologists as well as speech and language therapists working together or with the teachers at any one time. 'Working together' in such a context could apply to any combination of this multiprofessional team. For example, physiotherapists and speech and language therapists may find themselves working together regarding the children's posture and positioning as this will have a direct effect on communication and feeding, and the occupational therapist may be consulted with regard to feeding implements.

The availability of expertise and information from additional specialists within the school will have a positive effect on the teacher–speech and language therapist relationship in many ways as it extends their basic knowledge base and potential skills development. However, it may mean that there is a reduction in time available between the two of them for meetings and discussion.

Working together

Originally, in many special schools, teaching and therapy were kept separate within the timetable and no doubt teachers and therapists had few opportunities, or reasons, to work together. Now, however, every effort is made to integrate the children's therapy and education so that working together in the special school setting is essential. Indeed, as discussed in Chapter 5, one of the advantages of teachers working so closely with therapists is that therapy may become more compatible with the children's school work, and more relevant to other aspects of the children's academic studies. Conversely, therapy may be able to address specific difficulties which the children may be experiencing within the school programme. For example, if they are able to identify that the lack of underlying concepts is hindering one child's development within a specific subject area, they may agree that the therapist should undertake some specific concept work with that child, thus enabling the teacher to concentrate on the more general aspects of the subject area with the remainder of the class.

This is important if the children are to receive the type of curriculum to which they are entitled. Many children are able to cope with the National Curriculum, without need for its modification. However, the nature and form of some of the SATs mean that children with severe and complex problems may fail to pass the assessments. Despite this, staff in many special schools have accrued much experience in monitoring children's responses to teaching. Teachers often have specific skills in being able to assess children's progress in a manner which may then be utilised when drafting their IEPs.

Developments for staff by teachers and therapists

Some teachers have been able to disseminate and share their knowledge and skills through publishing their work, and this has been highlighted by Donlan (1986). He referred to the positive input of the professionals who worked closely in the residential setting of one of the I CAN special schools in Worthing, the John Horniman School, and the Moorhouse School, Oxted, Surrey, which cater for children with specific speech and language disorders. Such schemes as Language Through Reading (I CAN 1987), and The Colour Pattern Scheme (Lea 1970), which were developed by teachers while they were working at these schools, have made a significant contribution to the way in which teachers, and therapists, in many other settings are able to work with such children in relation to communication.

Similarly, teachers and therapists working together in Rowan School, a special school in Sheffield, have described their work with children with speech and language problems (Popple and Wellington 1996). Using a Psycholinguistic Framework (Stackhouse and Wells 1997) as a basis for their work, they describe ways in which they have successfully been able to bring therapy and education together in the classroom.

Working together within the classroom

The patterns of therapy intervention used for children with speech and language problems will vary in much the same way when working in special schools as when working with children in mainstream schools. Thus, children may be seen within the classroom, or withdrawn to a quiet, separate space for example, if work is needed specifically on attention control outside of the classroom. They may be seen individually, or work in small groups.

However, because there are often different approaches taken to teaching children in special schools, it is possible that many speech and language therapists will be able to work in different ways even within the classroom. For example, because of the smaller class sizes and the smaller ratio of children to adults, it may be possible for therapists to work with children individually, even within the classroom – provided that the other children do not prove to be too noisy, distracting or disruptive.

In other situations, a therapist may become part of a teaching session, specifically supporting individual children as the teacher works with the remainder of the class. Conversely, the teacher may involve the other class members in the therapy of specific children within the class, so that they are all able to benefit from some aspects of the therapy while supporting the individual children.

Teachers and speech and language therapists may also be able to work directly together, jointly planning and running specific activities which satisfy both educational and therapy aims. For example, they may agree that a primary focus for the class during one term is on the development of vocabulary, and this may be done within specific topics or themes. Then, both the teacher and therapist can decide on appropriate topics which are relevant to the long-term aims for the class. Together they will be able to choose the vocabulary to be used, adjust the level of the linguistic demands the work will make on children, and decide how they will introduce the topics and approach the teaching of the class. This joint focus from both educational and therapy points of view helps to provide a coherent context within which the children may learn. Within this overall framework, the professionals will be able to plan their aims for each of the children within individual sessions. This type of planning is particularly helpful if therapists only work part time within a school. It enables them to be aware of the topics or themes which will be used over a period of time by classes with which they are involved.

Social skills training is another area of development where the children may benefit from the teachers and therapists working directly together and where the whole class may be involved in work which is both educationally and therapeutically valid and pertinent for all the children. This may be achieved through programmes devised by the teachers and therapists or by use of a published programme such as the Social Use of Language Programme (Rinaldi 1992). Such work will be particularly relevant to children with pragmatic disorders who need to be able to generalise their knowledge and skills. If the resources are available it may be helpful for other adults working in the classroom to video such sessions so that the children may then be able to observe and reinforce their own 'good sitting and good listening'.

Planning and running such group sessions jointly may be beneficial in other ways, for example it may help the children to generalise the use of any of their newly acquired communication skills, some of which may have been introduced to them during individual therapy sessions.

Working together to run group sessions may enable the teacher and the therapist to alternate their time as group leader. This will enable the other to observe, assess, and make notes on individual children in relation to specific targets. For example, if they have a checklist of skills, one may observe and score the checklist, while the other leads the activity. It may be beneficial on occasion to repeat the task independently so that they may compare their rating skills as the basis for future discussions. This may enable them to map out their individual involvement in relation to their aims and objectives for future sessions. Of course, any non-teaching assistants may be included in this way so that the teacher and therapist may be free to observe and assess together.

Meetings

It must be recognised that it may not be easy either for an inexperienced therapist to work within a busy classroom or for an inexperienced teacher to present unfamiliar material in front of another professional. It is important, therefore, that both the teacher and therapist are sensitive to aspects of their joint work which each may find potentially difficult and to take time to learn how the other works. In order for their work within the classroom to be successful, teachers and therapists need time to become familiar with each others' ideas, materials and possible activities. Essentially they need time to meet and discuss, as a pair – which must be kept separate from any time they may spend together in more general meetings as members of a larger team.

It is helpful if a regular meeting time for the two of them can be established. In some schools, where such interactions are valued by the management and where working together is a recognised element of school policy, it may be possible to timetable such meetings, although more often they will need to be scheduled out of school hours at either end of the school day. The frequency, regularity and length of the meetings will naturally depend on the other commitments of each of the professionals, although it would be hoped that they could agree to meet for the minimum of half an hour several times a term. An agreed agenda may help to ensure that the meetings cover the issues which the pair consider essential to discuss.

Initially, it is crucial to establish what they consider to be their own specific needs, and to discuss their expectations, each of the other. As well as considering the specific problems of individual children, they will need to discuss their approaches to their work so that any differences may be aired and potential problems identified. They will need to address ways in which they consider that the work may be most satisfactorily shared; and to identify specific instances where they need to offer support to specific children. They will need to pool and share the results of any assessment findings and draw up together plans for future goals. It is helpful if they can find a way to share these aims with the parents concerned in order to ensure that intervention plans are cohesive. A copy of the joint aims – whether devised jointly, or devised individually and then mutually agreed – may be sent home regularly. Examples of their joint working practice may also be made available to parents during open days or parents' evenings, when the parents will have an opportunity to discuss their children with both of the professionals concerned.

When work is planned together and shared goals are identified, the ways in which these goals may be achieved will then become the focus for discussion. As Kersner and Wright (1996) found, this may help increase their commitment to the ensuing work. In addition, Wright (1994) found that both teachers and therapists considered that sharing their ideas and suggestions for future plans was both positive and exciting. This may be developed if opportunities arise for the teachers and therapists to attend courses, lectures or conferences together. They may find that the opportunity to share ideas and develop plans away from the classroom is stimulating and it may encourage them to think creatively about their work together.

It may also be interesting if the two professionals are able to share other external ventures such as visiting the current school of a child who may be transferring to their school. It is helpful to both if they are able to discuss their observations and findings together.

Of course it will be necessary, and helpful, to include in some meetings the other adults who share the workload in the classroom, and it will be important to schedule some larger meetings in addition to meetings between the pair. It will help all of the classroom assistants to understand the aims and objectives and in turn to engender feelings of commitment to their work.

Apart from meetings between the dyad, the need will remain for more formal multidisciplinary team meetings. The scheduling of such meetings may be dependent on the availability of the visiting medical specialist, for it is often the school's designated paediatrician or psychiatrist who leads such a team. Meetings of the multidisciplinary group are particularly important in relation to the annual reviews for each child, when all professionals involved share their reports on individual children. These are an important feature of all special schools and, although they often prove time-consuming, help all the staff to communicate and work cohesively.

Chapter 7

Current practice in special units

Introduction

As discussed in Chapter 6, special units may be available in some areas and they may be the preferred choice of education establishment of parents whose children have specific impairments. However, it is not always possible to accommodate all those children who desire places, as units covering each speciality are not available in all geographical areas, and the numbers of spaces for children within each unit are usually strictly limited.

Although the generic term 'unit' is used as a label for these specialist classes, units may vary in size and nature, from a 'class with a difference', to a 'mini' special school. In addition, they may each have different specifications and selection criteria, and may offer different educational and specialist expertise.

What is a unit?

In terms of structure and ethos a special unit is usually more closely related to a class in a mainstream school than a class in a special school, as indeed many are geographically attached to mainstream schools. If the unit is a part of the school, either geographically or administratively, then naturally the policies and the ways in which it is managed and run will be heavily influenced by the main school.

Many units cater for children who have a specific, predominant area of difficulty such as a physical impairment, or learning disabilities, and in this respect they are similar to special schools, providing separate, segregated education (Dessent 1987). However, there are some units which may be non-specialist, which have a sufficient number of pupils on their roll seemingly to constitute a small school, such as that described by Wade and Moore (1992).

One of the main features of special units is the small numbers of pupils within each class and the small ratio of pupils to adults. Donlan (1986), for example, reporting on language units, found that the ratio of teachers to children tended to be 1:8, with the addition in some cases of ancillary support staff within the classroom.

Aims of units

Essentially, units – like special schools – aim to combine education and therapy. By providing the resources, staff and expertise to cover a range of specific needs, the units are able to offer the children intensive intervention for their specific areas of difficulty. However, at the same time they enable access to mainstream education.

Within the units, the children have social contact with peers who may share similar areas of difficulty. In addition, most will also have some social contact, albeit less intensively, with their peers in mainstream schools. All of these experiences are gained, however, while the children are in a supportive and structured environment; an environment which, in the words of Webster and McConnell (1987), should provide 'a sense of continuity and act as a refuge for children who find the stresses and changes of a mainstream school daunting'. Jacklin and Lacey (1993) see the efficiency and effectiveness of the provision being influenced by the coordination of appropriate resources, and an integrated and coordinated multidisciplinary approach.

However, in many units the aim is to provide this modified form of special education for a specified and limited period only. Integration into mainstream schools is generally encouraged at some level, for it is this which will help the children to acclimatise to the mainstream environment – the setting to which most will eventually return. Hopefully a controlled and supported programme of integration will help them to prepare for eventual re-entry into mainstream education, although it is possible that some children may remain within the domain of special school provision.

Integration into mainstream

Most units are able to offer the children some level of integration within a mainstream school, although what is offered as a regular part of the timetable will vary. The level of integration will vary depending in part on the location of the school in relation to the unit, as this naturally will affect the children's potential frequency of attendance. For example, if the integrating school is geographically attached to the unit the children will be able to attend regularly; although if this is not the school to which the children will be returning, the effect of the integration may be reduced.

If children are integrated into local schools some distance from the unit, or attend some sessions within their original 'home' schools which may be in a different catchment area or borough, this, of necessity, would enforce less frequent attendance. The frequency and length of the integrating periods will also be partially dependent upon the ease with which compatible timetabling and course programming may be achieved between the units and the schools.

The amount of time spent by the children integrating into main schools will also vary according to the nature of the children's difficulties. Sometimes it may be more appropriate for children to spend most of their time within the unit, concentrating on the remediation of their specific difficulties and gaining the maximum use from the specialist teaching and special facilities. However, many children experience at least partial integration, which encourages social interaction and enables them to become involved in activities with their mainstream peers.

More successful integration may be encouraged if some of the teachers from the mainstream schools are able to teach some sessions within the units. This will enable them to understand the unit teachers' roles and expectations. They will also be able to observe for themselves the types of difficulties the children are experiencing so that they may then be able to plan more effective integration for the children from the unit who visit their own mainstream classrooms. A reciprocal arrangement, whereby the unit teachers are able to teach some sessions within the main schools (as described by Wade and Moore 1992), will also help to raise the awareness of the staff and children in mainstream schools about the special needs of the children in the units, and the work which is undertaken there.

There are often difficulties associated with the ultimate transition from the unit to the mainstream classroom at the end of the children's period spent at the unit. This may be greatly facilitated if the mainstream teachers understand the nature and the work which is undertaken in the units. Such difficulties may also be reduced by careful management of the children and the speedy transfer, for example, of records and information.

Types of units

The settings in which units were initially established – and have since been developed – vary greatly. For example, they may be self-contained, independent of any school; they may be attached to special schools, or to mainstream schools; or, children may attend their regular mainstream schools, being withdrawn for specific sessions – for example, sessions with teachers with special responsibilities for the children's area of difficulty, and with professionals such as speech and language therapists (Mobley 1987).

In relation to children with communication problems, special units are similar to special schools in that some units cater specifically for children for whom communication is their primary area of difficulty. Some units, on the other hand, are specifically designed for those whose communication difficulties are secondary, occurring as a result of primary cognitive, sensory, physical or emotional difficulties.

Units for children whose impaired communication is a secondary problem

There are specialised units throughout the UK which have been established for children with a variety of specific problems. For example, there are units for hearing impaired children, units for visually impaired children, units for children with physical disabilities, or for children with severe learning disabilities. Many of these are well established and cater for children across the age range. Within these units there will be children who have secondary communication difficulties, arising as a result of their primary impairments.

Speech and language therapy provision within such units for those children with associated communication problems will normally be similar to that described in Chapter 6 for children with similar problems who attend special schools. Teachers and speech and language therapists working together in such settings will probably experience similar benefits, and difficulties, to those described for the two professionals working in the special school system. Therefore, throughout the remainder of this chapter, the relationship between teachers and speech and language therapists working in such units will only be referred to specifically to highlight any appropriate, significant differences.

Units for children whose impaired communication is a primary problem

Units serving children with specific communication difficulties, however, do not necessarily function in the same way as special schools serving the same population, and many of the factors which influence the ways in which they work together are specific to the setting. The remainder of this chapter, therefore, will concentrate on the joint working practices between the teachers and speech and language therapists who work in those specialist units which were developed for children whose impaired communication is their primary problem – units which became known as 'language units'.

Language units

Language units which specialise in catering for children with primarily severe speech, language and communication difficulties have been developed since the late 1970s and they differ in many ways from special schools catering for such children. One important difference is that there is separate provision for primary-aged and secondary-aged children. Unfortunately, the majority of these units currently cater for primary school-aged children only. In some cases the upper age limit is nine, although some children may continue to attend until the age of eleven.

Many secondary-aged children who have attended primary-age units are able to rejoin their peers in the mainstream system. However, not all those who require further help will be able to attend units beyond this age as, despite new developments, there are still a comparatively small number of units available for secondary-aged children. Within the units which cater for older children, the focus of provision may differ from that in units providing for the younger age group. Often there is less emphasis on remediation and treatment of the communication disorders, the focus instead shifting to teaching the students coping strategies, social skills and study skills.

Those who may still require additional help and are unable to secure a place in units for secondary-aged children may move on to special schools.

Pre-school language units

During the 1970s there was a burgeoning of specialist provision for pre-school children with speech and language problems. It was hoped that children who received intensive help prior to school entry would be able to attend mainstream primary schools without additional support. This expectation was vindicated as a study by Urwin *et al.* (1988) demonstrated; for they found that 84 per cent of a group of eight year olds who had attended pre-school language units between the ages of three to five were making progress in mainstream education with little or no additional support. However, despite such encouraging figures there remains a significant number of children who continue to need support, and many of these will be found in primary-age language units.

Selection criteria

The entry criteria for language units will vary across the country and may even differ within a borough or education authority: as to date, there are no nationwide standardised criteria. In most authorities, criteria were established in order to meet the initial needs, and subsequently children were selected on the basis that they would effectively benefit from the teaching approach which had been developed within a specific unit. This means that language units throughout the country may have widely differing selection criteria for entry.

In a joint publication in 1996, The Association For All Speech Impaired Children (AFASIC) and I CAN attempted to address this problem by outlining specific principles for educational provision in relation to speech and language impaired children but no statutory standards or guidelines have yet been issued. However, in the majority of units, particularly those attached to mainstream schools, it is generally accepted that the children selected will have at least average non-verbal abilities and that the impaired/disordered speech and language will be the children's primary area of difficulty. There may be some children within units with additional problems and more complex needs, but normally these should be of secondary significance.

Staffing and support services

As referred to above, staffing levels within units are generally high in relation to the small numbers of children admitted. Usually the staff consists of teachers and speech and language therapists, and may include at least one non-teaching assistant and/or nursery nurse. Language units are unique within special educational provision as they are the only setting where there may often be an equal number of teachers and therapists employed to work with the children. In addition, because many units developed as a result of cooperation between health and education authorities, often both professionals share the same employer. For reasons previously discussed, this naturally will affect their working patterns and the ways in which they work together (see Chapters 1 and 3).

Of course, there are language units where this is not the case. There are many NHS employed speech and language therapists who only visit language units as a part of their duties. Or they may specialise in such work, visiting several units on a part time basis, fitting in with different teachers and their different ways of working. In these instances the professionals will face some of the difficulties previously outlined which may occur between dyads where the partners are working to different service level agreements and contracts (Jowett and Evans 1996), as discussed in Chapter 3.

Teachers may be appointed specifically to work in language units, or, if a unit is part of a mainstream school, they may be transferred directly from the main school to take responsibility for the attached unit. If this is the case, then it is possible that these teachers will not have the experience in working with children with such specific difficulties.

Specialisation

There is a statutory requirement that teachers who work in units which specialise in sensory impairments must have a specialist qualification. For example, within a unit for hearing impaired children the teachers are qualified teachers of deaf children (Lynas *et al*. 1997). However, it is not a statutory requirement for teachers working in language units to have a specialist qualification in language disorders. Nevertheless, like those who teach in special schools, some of the teachers in these special units do have additional qualifications and, over the years, many have now gained experience and expertise in the specific area of the children's difficulties. In the field of speech, language and communication disorders this covers a wide range of topics.

There is a popular misconception among some mainstream teachers that, because of the small class sizes and the high ratio of adults to children, the teachers who choose to work in language units have an 'easy option'. However, teachers working within units need a variety of different skills and knowledge, apart from their general education background and classroom management skills. For example, they need to acquire a working knowledge about the nature of speech and language; language development and breakdown, and the links between language and literacy; as well as of audiological management in relation to minor or intermittent hearing loss which may be affecting some of the children incidentally. They may also need to understand the visuo-spatial problems, perceptual difficulties, and the motor organisation and coordination problems which some of the children may have. If they are working with children with more complex needs, they may also need to learn how to implement and use an AAC system.

Given the breadth, and depth, of this potential corpus of knowledge, it is, perhaps, not surprising that there is an ever increasing number of teachers currently working with children who have speech and language problems who choose to avail themselves of the courses which are currently available for teachers* in order to increase their knowledge and skills in this specific field of work.

Although all speech and language therapists are by definition qualified

---

*In 1997, such courses are currently available at Birmingham, Newcastle, Sheffield and Kingston Universities.

to work with all children with communication problems, those who work in language units will usually try to gain specific expertise in working with children with specific language impairments. There are no accredited qualifications in this area available to them but there are post-qualification short courses, special interest groups recognised by the RCSLT and an increasing volume of literature relating to current research to which therapists wishing to develop their interests and specialism may turn. Therefore, it is not uncommon to find therapists who 'specialise' in working with the specific types of difficulties found in children who attend language units. Most often these specialist skills are similar to those developed by therapists working in special schools for children with specific language disorders.

Working together in a language unit

When therapists visit units regularly, but on a part time basis, the ways in which they may work together with the teachers will not be dissimilar to ways which have been discussed previously, particularly in Chapter 6. However, it is the fact that therapists may be working closely, on a full time basis, with only one or two teachers which is unique to the language unit setting. It is the relevance of this to their joint working practice, and the ways in which it may benefit and disadvantage the working relationship which will be the focus of the discussion below.

An additional factor which may affect the ways in which they work together is the influence of the mainstream schools, particularly if the units are physically attached or are close geographically to the schools. The management and organisation of the schools and the attitudes of their staff members, as well as the relationship of the unit based children to the children in the mainstream classes, will have at least a ripple effect – if not a more profound effect – on the way the units function and the manner in which they are managed and run.

Establishing joint aims

Because the teachers and therapists work so closely together in such a setting, it is particularly important for them to establish their aims together so that they have a shared understanding of what they are trying to achieve with the children, individually and collectively. This is seen as superordinate to the functioning of the whole unit (Withey 1991).

There are additional external pressures which affect the programmes designed for children within language units. Not least among these is the fact that there is an expectation that, ultimately, most of the children will return to mainstream classes, where it is hoped that they will be able to continue with their education without the need for further support. As referred to above, children who may still require additional help will be restricted in their choice of services because of the limited amount of secondary-age language unit provision which is currently available.

Another external pressure results from the shortness of the time they are allowed to spend within the units; for most children remain in language units for only a limited period, sometimes as little as two years, during which they are under great pressure to strive to achieve their full potential. The teachers and therapists are always keenly aware of the pressing need for the children to make as much progress as possible within this short space of time.

In order to facilitate the children when they return to mainstream education, the aims in relation to their communication skills will be twofold. The first aim will be that their speech and language should continue to develop and improve. The second aim will be to ensure that they are adequately equipped with coping strategies. This combination of skills may then enable the children to gain sufficient confidence for them to function independently within a broad-ranging social milieu, as well as within the mainstream education system.

Working in the classroom

Assessment and planning

With respect to the approach taken by teachers and speech and language therapists when assessing the children's needs and planning their individual education and therapy programmes, the same principles apply in language units as in other settings. The two professionals may choose to assess the children independently, possibly observing each other's specific procedures; they may then choose to pool their findings to facilitate their joint programme planning for each of the children. Or, they may decide to assess the children jointly to enable more cohesive planning.

Whatever their approach, it is the level of joint involvement which is critical in terms of their future working practices in relation to the children. For the greater the joint responsibility in the assessments, the more each can feel involved at the planning stage and, consequently, the greater their ultimate commitment is likely to be to the work which they will undertake with the children in the classroom.

Carrying out the programmes

If teachers and therapists are jointly employed to work full time within a unit, then they will have many opportunities to work together in the classroom. The amount of time they decide to spend working together directly in order to carry out their programmes will be influenced by the needs of the children. Thus, within the classroom, they may use many of the approaches described in Chapter 6. Or, they may use a team teaching approach which, as Pugach and Johnson (1995) suggest, is a valuable way of benefiting both pupils and professionals. However, as in special schools, on occasion it may be appropriate for each to focus on a specific aspect of the children's problems in different ways, so that the therapist may withdraw a child or a group of children and work with them separately, enabling the teacher to work with the same children using a different approach on another occasion.

Meetings and discussions

Because of their close proximity within the working environment, the teachers and therapists will have frequent opportunities for discussion. This may be facilitated if the classroom has an open plan configuration, which is common in many primary language units. Such a classroom layout will also enable each to observe the other's approach when working with the children so that explanations and specific demonstrations may be reduced to a minimum, or may even become redundant.

However, there will still be the need for more formal meetings to be held if, for example, long term and overall plans for the unit need to be discussed. These meetings will possibly include other members of staff, to enable them to become involved and to make their contribution. It may be important to spend some time in meetings looking at specific curriculum areas, identifying aims for the following terms or for the weeks ahead, as well as discussing detailed plans for the remainder of the current term. In addition, meetings will be needed so that the individual teaching and therapy plans may be drawn up in relation to specific assessments. During the term, meetings may be planned in order to review individual children, to discuss their progress generally, and to consider their performance in relation to specific targets which may have been set.

Whilst it is always necessary to hold meetings in order to deal with any problems and difficulties which may arise, it will also help morale within the unit if, at the same time, aspects of the work which are going well are also identified.

Keeping records

It is important for all teachers and therapists to keep records of the children with whom they are working in order to chart their progress. Good record keeping also facilitates communication with other staff members, informing them not only about the children's progress, but also about the aims and plans for each of the children individually and the class as a whole, so that they may be able to follow up specific aspects of the work as appropriate. Record keeping is an important two-way exchange of information even for professionals working closely together, ensuring that neither misses any important details regarding the children's progress and facilitating any member of staff who needs to stand in for another at short notice. Regularly updated records may also provide instant background material for annual reviews and requisite reports.

In the study by Wright (1994) some of the teachers and therapists interviewed talked of the importance of recording meetings, as well as recording the children's progress in the classroom. Whilst more formal minutes of the proceedings were preferred by some, there were others who considered their meetings to be their 'liaison time', so that they kept a 'liaison book' through which they could disseminate information to those who were unable to attend specific meetings.

Working with parents

Record keeping may also enable the teachers and therapists to compile reports regularly so that they may disseminate information to the parents of the children attending the language units, keeping them informed of their children's progress. This is particularly relevant if the children live some distance from the unit so that their parents are not able to visit often. Home-to-school books are also a useful way of keeping in touch. They may be completed by any adult who is working with the children both at the unit and at home, thus enabling a comprehensive exchange of information.

If parents are available to visit the school, the teachers and therapists may be able to jointly run courses for them, or to host special parents' evenings (mornings/afternoons). If regular meetings are possible this may allow them all to make use of approaches such as the Primary Language Record (Barrs *et al.* 1990) to which teachers, therapists and parents each contribute in order to develop a more complete profile of the children within their various communication contexts.

However, if the parents are unable to visit the school, it may be possible, if time allows, for the teachers and/or therapists to make occasional home visits instead.

Working in a language unit – the effects on the professional partnership of working in 'a goldfish bowl'

Potentially language units provide the ideal setting in which working relationships between teachers and speech and language therapists may develop and flourish. There, they are afforded a great number of opportunities to work together closely because of the nature of the staffing, the small numbers in the classes, and the specificity of the children's problems. Such closeness may be achieved particularly when the therapists work in the units on a full time basis, and many advantages and positive benefits may emerge as a result of the concerted effort between the professionals. However, it must be recognised that there may be some disadvantages to such exclusivity, as it may put unexpected strains on the professional partnership; for working within the confined space of a unit, has been likened by some to working in 'a goldfish bowl'.

The closeness of the proximity in which the small group of staff and children are normally required to work together throughout the week may contribute to feelings of claustrophobia. Indeed, some teachers and therapists have talked about feeling as if they were each 'shadowing' the other, or were 'joined at the hip'. However, unless the units are actually a part of the main school buildings, the unit staff will remain a small and exclusive group as they will not have many opportunities to interact regularly with the mainstream teachers. In addition, they may not easily be able to separate themselves from the children, even during break periods. It is possible, therefore, that instead of constantly seeking opportunities to meet, staff in such units may, from time to time, welcome the chance to spend some time apart, so that they may have the opportunity to work independently. This then may be reflected in the ways in which they choose to work with the children.

One strategy which may relieve this situation is for the unit teachers to have a role within the mainstream schools, or to extend their areas of responsibility into the schools. Developing such links with the host schools may have other advantages for the teachers on a more personal level, for there are limited opportunities for career development for teachers who remain solely within the restricted structure of the units. Therapists may benefit in a similar way from having some external professional interests or areas of responsibility. However, the amount of time spent away from the units would need to be mutually agreed, so that it does not in itself become a contentious issue.

Irrespective of whether they have a specific role in the main schools, it is nevertheless important for the unit staff to forge some links with the main school staff members and to ensure that there is effective liaison between the units and the schools. If the language unit teachers are able to build a good rapport with their mainstream teaching colleagues and feel supported by them, so that good working relationships may be developed between the unit staff and the school staff, this may help to reduce some of the claustrophobic effects of the unit.

When it becomes difficult for the unit staff to establish regular working contact with the main school teachers – either in terms of logistics, or because of personalities – it is not always straightforward to predict the effect on the partnerships within the units. If teachers feel isolated from their mainstream colleagues, they may look within the units for their sole support, and this may strengthen their partnerships with the therapists.

However, if this leads to one partner having too great a dependency on the other, then this may have a detrimental effect on the relationship as discussed below.

Similarly, the ways in which the speech and language therapists develop their relationships with the teachers will partly be dependent on the closeness of their working relationships with their speech and language therapy colleagues. Support from their external colleagues could give them additional confidence which may then enable them to work in close harmony with the teachers in the units. However, it is possible that, if therapists feel more strongly linked in their work with colleagues from their own profession, then this in turn may prove to be detrimental to their developing relationship with the teachers within the units.

One advantage of two professionals working so closely together is that they each have a sound working knowledge of all the classroom activities if one has a brief unplanned absence. However, there will be some additional benefits if the pair are also able to organise some degree of separation. For when two people work closely together successfully, they each become extremely difficult to replace, should one of them leave. If they have been completely reliant on each other within the work place, the one remaining would, no doubt, find it difficult to begin to develop a new partnership. Thus, they would both benefit from having the opportunity to work with other colleagues as well, so that they would be better prepared to make the necessary adjustments to working with a new partner should the need arise.

Another feature of this close partnership which has both positive and negative aspects is the definition of roles. In some units there is an overlap of roles between the teachers and the therapists such that it may become difficult to define the boundaries between the two. This may be seen positively, for example, in terms of understanding all classroom procedures. However, in various aspects of their work it may be unclear who is responsible for what, and who should be taking the lead role at any given time. Not only has lack of clarity of roles been found to be stressful (Dunham 1992), but it could also lead to friction within the unit if there are no clearly defined boundaries of areas of responsibility in relation to the children's speech and language problems, and tensions could arise if the workload is not carefully apportioned.

One factor which would obviously contribute to the 'goldfish bowl' effect, is being observed by others; a phenomenon which affects the staff and children in language units perhaps more than in any other comparable setting. For, as the expertise of the staff develops, the units will be recognised by the schools, and possibly by the LEAs, as a valuable resource; a resource which needs to be promoted. Such units may then become the focus of interest for other professionals, and parents of prospective entrants, many of whom will wish to visit. Of course it is important to enhance the reputation of the language units and to raise awareness about the innovative approaches to communication needs which are so often developed by staff within such settings. However, having a stream of visitors may put untold strain on the children as well as on the best of staff relationships.

In the main, most partnerships, however slowly, develop in strength over time, benefiting not only from their joint work with the children, but also from the ways in which they each contribute to the development of their own working relationship. A particularly difficult situation to resolve may result if an initially successful partnership does not continue to develop, and then begins to fail. Within the close confines of a language unit, one of the professionals may feel that it is more appropriate to leave the unit than to continue working in acrimony. For it can become difficult for the children if the professionals are not ultimately able to compromise and adapt to each other's ways of working.

Personalities, of course, are a key factor when working so closely together. There can be no room within units for unresolved conflicts or smouldering resentments. In order for successful working practices to develop, any potential clashes or personality differences have to be confronted so that the professionals find some way in which they may be able to continue working together.

Naturally, different partnerships will be affected in different ways, even by the same pressures, dependent upon the personalities of the professionals concerned and the specific setting. Thus, as already demonstrated above, whether the resultant effect is positive or negative will vary in each individual situation so that what is stress for one pair may be distress for another.

This may also be true for example, for some dyads, who work together all the time in the same classroom, constantly discussing their aims for the children, planning and working together from the beginning to the end of each school day. This may lead one or both of them to feel smothered and overwhelmed. Another pair, however, could view the same situation positively, feeling exhilarated by such a working partnership, so that they are able to give and take constantly without feeling that their own strength and resources have been depleted. Rather, they may feel that they are stimulated to produce a higher quality of work together than either may be able to produce individually.

Chapter 8

Developing the relationship

Introduction

Initially when any two professionals begin working with the same children there is the potential for each to 'deal with [their] own "bit" of the client'. This could mean that 'without co-ordination, gaps and/or overlap in services are likely to occur', and each can blame the other for any difficulties which may arise (Roberts 1994). Such situations could arise for example, as discussed in Chapter 4, when children who have been the sole responsibility of one agency (speech and language therapy) first attend school, and thus become the school's responsibility, under the jurisdiction of the LEA (Dick 1994).

This, however, can be prevented if the two are able to take a harmonised and coordinated approach as has been discussed in previous chapters in relation to research evidence such as that of Reid *et al.* (1996); Kersner and Wright (1996); Wright (1994) and ASHA (1991). Roberts (1994) also concurs with this view, for she goes on to state unequivocally that, 'working well together . . . is generally considered a good thing', and that well managed relationships, 'can do much to improve morale and effectiveness in the human services'.

If, as the literature suggests, successful working partnerships are potentially so worthwhile, it seems reasonable that professionals such as teachers and speech and language therapists should concentrate some of their resources on the development of a joint working approach.

However, despite the fact that working together may ultimately produce beneficial results – for the professionals and for the children – it must be recognised that this is not an easy option. For, as Lacey and Lomas (1993) point out, it is one thing to identify the need for an integrated and unified approach to pupils with special educational needs, but it is quite another to develop such an approach successfully. Successful partnerships generally are the result of much hard work. In order to demonstrate this, this chapter will focus on the nature of working partnerships which may develop between teachers and therapists, following the process from its initial stages through its development over time.

Working together – prerequisites

As with any relationship, the ways in which working partnerships between teachers and therapists develop and evolve is the responsibility of the individuals concerned. In order for them to be successful, the teachers and therapists need to demonstrate their commitment to joint working practice. The respective partners must show that the success of the relationship is of sufficient importance to each of them that they are willing to invest time and energy in its development; in the constant discussion and negotiation, and possibly the training, which will be needed so that they can exploit their own and each others' skills and experiences for their mutual benefit.

However, commitment, dedication and goodwill are not sufficient in isolation to ensure that good joint working practice automatically ensues. A working relationship can only develop successfully if it is built on firm foundations. For as Loxley (1997) points out: 'in order to succeed, practitioners . . . require sufficient knowledge, a repertoire of relevant skills, appropriate structures for the exchange of information and resources and processes which facilitate relationships . . .' and that '. . . no one of these is sufficient, all are necessary.'

For example, it is important to establish the knowledge base which each of the pair has of the other's profession, such as that outlined by Fleming *et al.* (1997). For if they do not clearly understand how they each spend their time apart, then this is a potential area for conflict and confusion when they try to prioritise their work together within the context of their overall workload.

Thus, teachers may assume that the speech and language therapists with whom they work will not only gather specific information about the schools in which they are working but also about the ways in which teachers function in the modern education system and currently work in the classroom, and that they will have considered some of the implications for their therapy in the educational setting.

Similarly, teachers may be expected to be informed about the overall work and difference of approach taken by therapists, and the specific factors regarding therapy in education which must be taken into account if they are to work together. Such information in the initial stages of a partnership may prevent the pair from having erroneous and unrealistic expectations of each other, so ensuring that the relationship does not begin on rocky foundations.

Some teachers, such as support teachers, may have a good understanding of the work of therapists and be well acquainted with therapy approaches, some of which may have much in common with their own work. Indeed, by the nature of their more specialised work, many support teachers – in particular those who work peripatetically – may share a closer affinity to therapists than to class or subject teachers and this will naturally affect their working relationships (Reid *et al*. 1996).

It is also important for teachers and speech and language therapists to be aware of possible differences in the ways in which they respectively work with parents. This will be particularly relevant, as referred to above, when the therapist has been involved with a child prior to school entry and has already established a relationship with the parents.

In addition to knowledge and skills, they will both need to demonstrate their tenacity and determination to continue working at the relationship, for within an enduring partnership the professionals will be involved in prolonged cooperative activity requiring constant compromise and accommodation. Protracted periods of contact in any partnership brings their own pressures, irrespective of the nature of that contact, whether they are working closely together in the same classroom or the same school, or are merely maintaining good lines of communication, for example through regular telephone contact.

The stresses and strain of this continuous adjustment and readjustment will naturally be reduced if the dyad are working within a supportive management structure and a conducive environment and this will be discussed further below. However, perhaps the saving grace for any professionals – and any working relationship – will be the maintenance of a positive attitude and a sense of humour!

Working together – the early stages

If working partnerships are to develop, it is important that the 'task' on which the dyad are jointly focussed is not only clear to both of the professionals involved, but that that task appears feasible and manageable to them both. In addition, it is important that any aims, goals and priorities which they jointly agree are not in conflict with the aims or priorities of either of the professionals. They will need to set a 'superordinate goal over and beyond the goals for each professional group' (Loxley 1997), for, initially at least, they will be strongly influenced by the motivations of their individual professions, which by their very nature are bound to differ.

For example, teachers will be motivated towards educating the children, and enabling them to perform well on the within-school assessments and public examinations. Therefore, their primary focus will be to help the children access the subjects within the National Curriculum. Speech and language therapists, on the other hand, will be motivated by the desire to equip all the communication impaired children with a means of functional communication, so that their first priority will be to ensure that the children are able to express their needs and make themselves understood.

However, such differences need not preclude their working together, or developing a jointly motivated task. Indeed working relationships may be enhanced by what Loxley (1997) refers to as '[an] enrichment of diversity and the reconciliation of difference' which may be made possible by the differing values and attitudes of the pair. What is required is a process of identification of shared goals, and clarification of the means by which these will be achieved.

Not surprisingly, in order for such agreement to be reached, and for their joint task to be realised effectively, much careful negotiation will be required. For example, with children who have difficulties applying their communications skills to a social setting the teacher may feel that it is more appropriate for the therapist to work separately with such children outside of the classroom. However, the therapist may feel that while it may be possible for appropriate strategies to be targeted within the structure and safety of a one-to-one setting, it will be easier for the children to learn how to use their communication skills in a group situation, within a social setting such as the classroom. The teacher and therapist, therefore, need to consider their overall goals in the light of these differences of approach, and negotiate from their respective positions about how these goals may best be achieved. A compromise will need to be reached, possibly enabling the skills to be established through withdrawal sessions, but allowing them to be put into group practice within the context of the classroom.

From the beginning, however, it is important not only that they each feel that they are able to make a specific – and necessary – contribution to the work in which they are jointly involved, but that this contribution is explicitly valued and acknowledged each by the other. This may be of particular significance in relation to newly qualified professionals, as discussed further below.

Working together – but separately

Of course, it must be acknowledged that there may be some teachers and therapists working in the same school who actually do not wish to develop a close working relationship. They may interact well socially so that within the school there may be an assumption that they are working closely together when in fact they are not. They may be merely working alongside each other, in parallel, making no attempt to share common goals or activities. This may be for a variety of reasons, including fear of personality clashes which they may both recognise; time constraints, or other conflicting external factors which one or both are not prepared to overcome.

In such instances it is important that the teachers and therapists themselves should recognise the disparate nature of their working relationship, so that they are not expecting the natural evolution of a closer partnership to occur.

The development of the relationship

As with all relationships, working partnerships which do develop only do so over time, during which as problems are encountered they may be resolved and overcome. Such resolution may be the result of specific discussion and problem solving undertaken by the pair, but it will also be influenced by the continuous interactional process which is an integral part of any organic relationship; that is, the constant adjustment and accommodation to each other which each will be required to make.

Adjustment to external changes, such as those within the broader environs of the NHS and the education system outlined in previous chapters, as well as to the effects of the internal dyadic process, requires flexibility and adaptability on the part of the professionals. They need to keep abreast of current issues which may affect either or both of them professionally; to be prepared to reconsider their attitude or adjust their approach in response to these external changes; and to be open to new ideas. If there is a climate of trust between them then the teacher and therapist will be able to work comfortably together, and will be prepared, where necessary, to hand over responsibility when working with the children, one to the other (Loxley 1997). Flexibility about their respective roles will hopefully then remove the potential for rivalry and conflict so that they will be able to think creatively about developing activities aimed at their common goal.

It is important that no professional jealousy or envy occurs between the teachers and therapists so that one is never in a position to 'blame' the other, as such elements could prove destructive to their relationship. On the contrary, within their joint working practice they must each take an equal share of the responsibility so that the 'power' – both perceived and actual – within the partnership remains finely balanced between them and the pleasures of success as well as the disappointment of failures are equally shared. However, above all, they must maintain a high level of sensitivity to each other and their respective needs, for in a dynamic relationship these needs also change as the relationship develops.

Some problems – intrinsic to the pair – may disappear through a process of natural resolution, while others, seemingly resolved, may be revisited, possibly in a mutated form. For example, a teacher may find it difficult to accept that the therapist is never available on a Friday afternoon because of speech and language therapy departmental meetings. A compromise may be struck that the therapist will be available on occasion by attending the therapy meetings on alternate weeks. However, further difficulties may arise, similarly in relation to conflicting professional demands, if the therapist then arrives late on several occasions because of supporting another therapist concerning a specific child in a health centre. The issue of priorities in the face of divided professional loyalties will need to be confronted by the pair again. Similarly, negotiations would need to take place with the teacher if the therapist were unable to have access to specific children because they were involved in rehearsals for the school play.

It is, of course, not surprising that Reid *et al.* (1996) found evidence of conflict about cross team membership and divided loyalties between the members of the different professions. For this is particularly common in the early stages of a developing working partnership as initially they each tend to define themselves in terms of their 'home group' (Roberts 1994). At times this may make it difficult for the dyad to work effectively together, particularly if the division in loyalties becomes competitive.

However, as the pair gradually invest more in their own partnership and begin to build a shared value-system, so their joint aims and tasks should begin to take on more meaning. As there is a shift in the emotional significance of their work together, so they usually become more committed to the aims of their joint work even to the extent of 'forgetting' their allegiance to their 'home group' membership (Roberts 1994).

This is most likely to happen on the part of therapists as they begin to spend more time working with the teachers in schools, away from their 'home group'. Indeed, there are some therapists whose work experience may be entirely, or predominantly, within the education system, where they may perhaps have been employed by an LEA or a school. Consequently they may remain committed to education, and feel that NHS issues are less relevant to them.

Nevertheless, Roberts (1994) feels that it is an important aspect of a working partnership that professionals are able to manage and carefully balance their membership of their own profession with that of the dyad. It is important for them to maintain their individual integrity because within the dyad each represents the interests of their own professional group. In fact, the effectiveness of the pair depends on this dual membership and the linking function across the professions. For, as Roberts goes on to say, excessive commitment to one membership at the expense of the other 'will inevitably compromise task performance', and it may lead to problems within their own group – that is, with other therapists.

Contrary to one of the fears expressed by teachers and therapists in the Reid *et al.* (1996) study, it would not be beneficial to either of the professionals if their work became generic, their differences denied. For success within the dyad and with the children depends not on the total merging and obliteration of their differences in skills, training and experience, but in encouraging them to exploit to the full their own special skills, particularly those which are profession specific (Roberts 1994).

Factors affecting the process

There are external factors which naturally affect the development of any working partnership; factors such as the stress of having a limited amount of time together for meetings, as discussed in Chapter 4. Conversely, there is also the possibility that dyads may suffer from 'too much togetherness' (Roberts 1994), such as in language units where the 'goldfish bowl effect' may occur as referred to in Chapter 7.

However, there are also many factors arising from within the dyad – from the nature of the relationship itself – which influence the course of its development. For example, the impetus for the continual development of the relationship may come directly from within the dyad, from the ways in which the pair stimulate and motivate each other in their work. Reid *et al.* (1996) found in their Scottish study that, often, it was seeing the progress which resulted from their initial attempts to work together that encouraged staff to continue to develop their joint approach.

In the studies by Reid *et al.* and Wright (1994), teachers and therapists themselves identified factors which contributed towards the development of their successful relationships; factors such as mutual respect, motivation, common goals and regular contact. Wright also found that when interviewed, teachers and speech and language therapists who were working together were easily able to identify ways in which their working partnerships could be improved.

For example, some teachers felt that their relationships with therapists would be enhanced if they (the teachers) understood more about the language assessments which the therapists used. Some of the therapists, on the other hand, identified that they needed more opportunities for observation in the classroom and an increased knowledge of teaching strategies in order to improve their relationships with teachers. These views are supported by the work of Sanger *et al.* (1995) who surveyed the opinions of educators about speech and language services in schools in the USA. They found that by learning about curricular and classroom management techniques therapists were able to work together more successfully with the educators.

The previous experience of each of the professionals: their life experience; their working experience, and their past experiences of working in a close dyadic relationship will naturally affect their attitudes to their current partnerships and will influence the ways in which they work together with others. Thus, the respective maturity and ages of any pair who are working together – as well as their gender, and previous work situations – will often have an effect on their joint working practices. Such factors will influence their expectations of their roles and the ways in which they may relate within the dyad.

For example, if there is a significant age difference between the pair, the older one of the two may take a 'parenting' role and may appear authoritarian or even condescending to a younger colleague. On the other hand, the younger of the two could feel superior, feeling more 'up to date' in terms of skills and technological expertise. In the same way, a mixed-gender pairing may find that contentious attitudes and opinions which could affect their relationships may differ from those which would affect a same-gender pairing so that expectations of others from outside of their partnership may strongly influence their own relationship. Similarly those who have had difficulties working with a previous partner will no doubt be influenced by their past experience and will be more cautious about taking the initiative in a new partnership. Whatever the differences between the pair, each of these issues need to be addressed within the individual dyad in order for the relationship to develop and grow successfully.

Another aspect of their previous life experience – and work experience – which teachers and therapists bring to their joint work is the different knowledge base which emerges from their respective professions and the different sets of basic assumptions from which they each operate. For, according to Crepeau (1991), individuals draw inferences and interpret new experiences based on their 'knowledge schemata' – their preconceived ideas and beliefs; their individual-specific experiences. Tannen and Wallet (1986) point out that these knowledge schemata often change little during interaction. Therefore they must be explicitly explored and any differences discussed so that potential conflict may be avoided.

Thus, for example, some teachers may not necessarily understand the underlying pathology of language disorder and may consequently hold the mistaken belief that environmental factors are the sole cause of children's communication difficulties. This could then lead to a teacher's false assumption that, given sufficient therapy and appropriate teaching input, the children's speech and language will develop normally. The therapist would need explore – and attempt to change – such knowledge schemata in order for their joint work with the children to be successful.

Similarly, it is equally difficult for teachers if therapists believe that the only way to teach children to read is via reading schemes, using a phonological approach which incorporates rhyming, sound awareness and phonics. The teacher would need to try to convince the therapist that it would be more helpful for some of the children if the teaching also included reading from 'real' books and a greater dependence on the use of context.

Misunderstandings between the professionals may arise not only from differences in knowledge schemata but also from the use of language itself, as discussed previously, for example, in terms of different interpretations of the word 'language' and the technical use of words such as 'pragmatics' (see Chapters 3 and 4). However, both professionals need to ensure that they do not use 'jargon' and that all terms are clarified as misunderstandings may arise inadvertently (Reid et al. 1996). For example, a therapist may offer a child 'regular therapy'. But how often is 'regular'? The teacher may assume that this means once a week and plan accordingly; whereas the therapist may understand it differently; in terms of speech and language therapy service delivery, regular could mean once a month, or it could mean every day but only for one term per year!

Another important factor which will influence the development of the relationship between a teacher and a therapist is the involvement of a third person. Then, the effects will be dependent in part on the levels of experience and maturity of each of the three comprising the 'triad', as well as on the existence of a previous close working relationship between any two of the threesome. Thus, for example, a new working partnership may begin to develop between an experienced teacher and a relatively inexperienced therapist. However, the development of such a partnership would be affected if there had been a previous long-standing, close working relationship in the classroom between the teacher and an equally experienced non-teaching assistant. On the other hand, the development of a teacher–therapist dyad and the way in which the triad worked together would be different if the teacher and therapist, both relatively inexperienced, had to work with an experienced assistant who was likely to outstay them within the classroom.

The ways in which any triadic relationship evolves will depend on several different factors, including how the classroom is organised in terms of hierarchy, lines of authority and roles; and to what extent the assistant is involved in decision making, planning, and carrying out tasks with the children. In addition, it will be important for the role of the assistant within the classroom to be clarified, and for the teacher and therapist to acknowledge the potential effects this may have on the development of their own professional relationship. If the assistant is involved in supporting communication impaired children within the classroom, adjustments within the triad will need to be made to ensure that all three are able to work effectively for the children.

Another example of how a third person may play a key role within their partnership is when therapists need to maintain telephone contact with teachers between their visits to the schools. As teachers rarely have access to a telephone during school hours, this will often mean that the pair have to rely on the goodwill of the school secretary in order for their own communication lines to work effectively. In addition, the teachers and therapists not only need to ensure the confidentiality of their discussion, but must also feel comfortable about their own telephone interpersonal skills and confident that they can adapt those skills appropriately to ensure that all such calls are succinct and businesslike without being abrupt.

Supervision

Even the most competent professionals may, at times, have doubts about their effectiveness, and become too involved with the children and their problems, as well as with the internal 'politics' of the classroom and the school. This is particularly true for any professionals whose work requires them to give much of themselves emotionally, such as teachers and therapists working with communication impaired children. In addition, professionals working in education and health have experienced considerable change within their working environment in recent years (see Chapter 1) which has often resulted in unacceptable levels of stress. They have had to adapt to new technological systems and information, to develop new skills, and to streamline their services in response to the changes in the economic climate. The experience of change on such a scale within the workplace often leaves professionals feeling anxious, deskilled, inadequate, and isolated, and in their own words 'in need of support' (Wright 1994).

Within many helping professions, support is often available from within the management structure, although research has shown that both teachers and therapists find it more helpful to be able to discuss and share problems with colleagues, either individually or within support groups (Dunham 1992; Kersner and Stone 1990). However, for teachers and therapists who are not only sharing the emotional stress of working with communication disordered children but are also trying to develop a functionally effective, close working partnership it may be helpful if they are able to receive support from someone outside of their immediate situation, through supervision.

Non-managerial supervision

Hawkins and Shohet (1989) recommend that supervisory support, either through individual supervision or through support groups, should be used by all professionals whose work involves the care of others. For supervision enables helpers to take care of themselves, and plays an important part in their ongoing self development, providing them with a means of maintaining a high level of self awareness and an openness to learning. The benefits of supervision are two-fold, for it provides professionals with an opportunity to stand back and reflect on their working relationships, as well as on their work with the children, thus enabling them to look at their interactions both with other professionals and with their clients.

A formal arrangement of supervision with someone other than their line managers is recommended by RCSLT (1996) for speech and language therapists, as a means of preventing over-emotional involvement with the children, whilst reinforcing and affirming the therapists' professional role. Dunham (1992), writing about teachers, shows that supervision may enable teachers to function more effectively by helping them come to terms with the stress and pressures of the classroom.

Supervision may also be important in maintaining good working relationships with all colleagues in the work place for, when under stress, communication channels are often the first to suffer. Those who are stressed act out their frustration and anxieties on their fellow workers so that they become irritable with the secretary, angry with their boss and non-cooperative with working partners, irrationally disagreeing over areas of responsibilities so that erstwhile cohesive teams may suddenly become fragmented. This may be particularly pertinent within schools, for example in split-site secondary schools, or in language units which are situated in large primary schools, or even in large special schools, where the maintenance of good communication between all the professionals involved with individual children is crucial.

Supervision of the 'process'

Wright (1996) suggests that when teachers and therapists first begin to work together it is helpful if a qualified supervisor – or even a mutually acceptable colleague – acts as a facilitator for their 'collaborative process'. Thus, within a supervision session they may be able not only to discuss the difficulties they are encountering as a result of their work together, but also to identify some of the ways in which they may be personally and professionally benefiting from the partnership. They will have the opportunity to stand back and take an objective view of their work together; to reflect on the process of their developing relationship, and to identify their own learning processes as well as any specific knowledge which they may have gained.

Supervision may prevent those involved in developing close working relationships from seeking to 'blame' others – or themselves – if things go wrong; it may offer them additional opportunities for learning, even from the most difficult situations; and provide a relevant forum within which to consider new options. It can help to prevent the feelings of staleness, rigidity and defensiveness which can ultimately contribute to the extreme symptom of stress known as 'burnout'; and enable the professionals to leave behind feelings of guilt and inadequacy so that they can concentrate on maintaining and improving their work standards.

Naturally, within a supervision session they will also have the opportunity to analyse in detail any difficulties which may have arisen between them. A supervisor may help them to tease out the issues, attempt to solve the problems or, in some instances, help them to reconstrue a problem to enable them to see a possible solution. For example, a therapist who is working regularly with assistants in the classroom regarding the children with communication problems may find it difficult to arrange a time to meet with the teacher. Thus, if the teacher is occupied with the needs of the other children in the class, it may not be possible for the therapist to feed back information about the activities, strategies and discussions which take place each week. The therapist may then become increasingly frustrated by this lack of communication with the teacher.

One seemingly obvious solution may be for the teacher and therapist to agree on some specific meeting times, even if they are brief and less frequent than the therapist initially envisaged. However, a supervisor may enable the pair to 'reframe' the difficulty by asking the therapist to identify why it seems so important to report back to the teacher so often, and why it is not sufficient to share the information mainly with the assistant who works closely with the teacher at other times. It may be possible that the therapist and teacher will then see the problem from a different perspective, and they may agree that regular meetings between the two of them are not so important. They may even come to the conclusion that a more beneficial solution is for them both to ensure that the assistant is fully enabled to bridge the communication links between them.

Of course teachers and therapists may well argue that supervision would be merely an additional burden within their already crowded schedules. They may feel that they cannot justify the luxury of taking time out to reflect on their working partnership – but the question must be asked: if they are to succeed, can they afford not to?

Supporting the newly qualified professional

When working with communication impaired children, there is no less an expectation for newly qualified teachers and therapists to work closely together than there is for their more experienced counterparts. However, such demands may be unrealistic, for the issues which arise between any two professionals trying to work closely together (as discussed above) will, almost inevitably, be more exaggerated among newly qualified professionals. For example, Dunham (1992) feels that for teachers the first year is often particularly stressful as they are not only new to the profession but also new to the school, unfamiliar with their surroundings and the organisational procedures. In addition, newly qualified teachers and therapists often find it difficult to define and establish their professional role which may not be clear cut, and this provides an additional stress factor with which they may need help (Hawkins and Shohet 1989; Dunham 1992).

Responses by newly qualified therapists to a survey conducted within an LEA indicated that they lacked confidence in their knowledge and abilities. They felt vulnerable, afraid of 'being found out'. They also felt that they lacked negotiating skills and the ability to assert themselves in order to get their needs met. However, these therapists were then supported by more experienced staff members when they began working in primary and/or secondary mainstream schools as part of a project undertaken within the LEA (Roux 1996).

It is particularly important for professionals to experience good supervision at the beginning of their professional careers. Then the 'habit' of receiving good supervision becomes an integral part of their work life and their continuing professional development (Hawkins and Shohet 1989).

Continuing professional development

There are many other aspects of continuing professional development which are important for teachers and therapists as well as supervision, and this is acknowledged when they begin to seek ways to improve and develop their working relationships. As has been discussed above, it is imperative for all professionals to keep pace with the considerable changes and developments which have occurred in their working environment and, through the process of continuing professional development, they may continue to increase and update their knowledge, and to develop and refine their existing skills – or learn new ones – which may then be used within the work place.

There are several ways in which this process may occur. For example, many teachers and therapists become engaged in their own individual continuing professional development, almost inadvertently, as soon as they begin to develop their joint working practices. For, as Wright (1996), Kersner and Wright (1996) and Reid *et al.* (1996) reported, teachers and therapists felt that their skills and knowledge base began to develop and expand as a result of working together. However, while some professionals within a dyad or a team have opportunities to learn from each other, others must actively seek out specific ways in which to enhance their knowledge and skills for example, by attending courses, conferences or through reading professional journals and books.

Continuing to develop the professional relationship

It is also important that professionals working closely together in a dyad or team are able to extend their professional development and receive some form of additional training in relation to the development of their working relationship. For it cannot be assumed that they will acquire the collaborative skills required in order to develop a successful professional partnership from their first level of professional training. The skills needed to work together are not an integral part of the initial training and education of teachers or therapists, so that it cannot be assumed that either will know how best they may work together; nor that they will understand automatically the potential benefits to joint working practices.

The need for continuing professional development for such purposes was highlighted by Reid *et al.* (1996) who found that a lack of training in cooperative or collaborative working was one of the factors which often prevented successful partnerships developing, for there are some professionals who, without guidance, do not perceive of themselves as 'team players'. Higgin *et al.* (1992), four therapists who also trained as teachers, suggest additionally that both professional groups would benefit if there were increased liaison between those responsible for training teachers and therapists, as this too would facilitate a 'reciprocal understanding' between the two professions. Thus it may be helpful if there were some opportunities, for example through courses, in which professional development may be pursued jointly. This idea is supported by Prelock *et al.* (1995) in the USA who suggest that collaborative in-service training may be a helpful way of approaching the question of continuing professional development.

Spreading the word

Through continuing education, professionals will be able, not only to acquire further skills and knowledge and increase their understanding about their professional partners, but will also have the opportunity to raise the awareness of others about their own profession. Hopefully, this will result in both professionals becoming more skilful in the ways in which they work together and will provide opportunities for them to disseminate to a wider audience the benefits of working in such a way.

The more they are able to spread the word, the more the children in their care will continue to benefit.

References

AFASIC and I CAN (1996) *Principles for educational provision for children and young people with speech and language impairments.* London: Association for all Speech Impaired Children and I CAN.

Almond, K. (1997) 'A view from the other side of the desk', *RCSLT Bulletin* **545**, 8–9.

ASHA (1991) 'A model for collaborative service delivery for students with language–learning disorders in public schools', *American Speech–Hearing Association* **33**, 44–50.

Axelrod, R. (1984) *The evolution of co-operation.* New York: Basic Books.

Barrs, M., Ellis, S., Hester, H. and Thomas, A. (1990) *Patterns of learning.* London: Centre for Language in Primary Education.

Blau, P. (1986) *Exchange and power in social life.* Oxford: Transactions Publications.

Bloom, L. and Lahey, M. (1978) *Language development and language disorders.* New York: John Wiley and Sons.

Catts, H. W. (1996) 'Defining dyslexia as a developmental language disorder', *Topics in Language Disorders* **16**(2) 14–19.

Conoley, J. C. and Conoley, C. W. (1982) *School consultation: a guide to practice and training.* Oxford: Pergamon.

Conoley, J. C. and Conoley, C. W. (1992). *School consultation: practice and training* (2nd edn). Boston, Mass.: Allyn and Bacon.

Cooke, J. and Williams, D. (1985) *Working with children's language.* Bicester: Winslow Press.

Crepeau, E. B. (1991) 'Achieving intersubjective understanding: examples from an occupational therapy session', *The American Journal of Occupational Therapy* **45**, 1016–25.

Cunningham, C. and Davis, H. (1985) *Working with parents: frameworks for collaboration.* Milton Keynes: Open University Press.

Daines, B., Fleming, P. and Miller, C. (1996) *Spotlight on SEN: speech and language difficulties.* Tamworth: NASEN Publications.

Dale, N. (1996) *Working with families of children with special needs.* London: Routledge.

DES (1970) The Education (Handicapped Children) Act. London: HMSO.

DES (1981) Education Act. London: HMSO.

DES (1988) Education Reform Act. London: HMSO.

DFE (1993) Education Act. London: HMSO.

DFE (1994) *Code of Practice on the Identification and Assessment of Special Educational Needs.* London: HMSO.

DFE (1996) Education Act. London: HMSO.

Department of Education (1945) *The Handicapped Pupils and School Health Service Regulations.* London: HMSO.

Department of Health (1973) Reorganisation of the Health Service Act. London: HMSO.

Dessent, T. (1987) *Making the ordinary school special.* London: Falmer Press.

Dick, M. (1994) 'The school health service', in Solity, J. and Bickler, G. (eds) *Support services: issues for education, health and social service professionals.* London: Cassell.

Donlan, C. (1986) 'Profiles of integration – the variation between language units', in *Advances in working with language disordered children.* Conference Paper. London: ICAA.

Donlan, C. (1992) 'Basic numeracy in children with specific language impairment', *Child Language Teaching and Therapy* **9**, 95–103.

Dunham, J. (1992) *Stress in Teaching.* London: Routledge.

Edwards, A. and Talbot, R. (1994) *The hard pressed researcher: a handbook for the caring professions.* Harlow: Longman.

Figg, J. and Stoker, R. (1989) 'A school consultation service: a strategy of referral management leading to a second order change', *Educational and Child Psychology* **6**, 34–42.

Fleming, P., Miller, C. and Wright, J. (1997) *Speech and language difficulties in education: approaches to collaborative practice for teachers and speech and language therapists.* Bicester: Winslow Press.

Garner, P. (1994) '"Oh, my God help": what newly qualifying teachers think of special schools', in Sandow, S. (ed.) *Whose special need?* London: Paul Chapman Publishing.

Geliot, J. (1993) *Supporting speech and language impaired children in the classroom. A training manual for teachers and classroom assistants.* Canterbury and Thanet Community Health Care Trust.

Graham, J. (1995) 'Interprofessional collaboration in the special school'. Unpublished PhD thesis. London: Institute of Education.

Hall, R. (1990) *Talking Together.* Northumberland: STASS Publications.

Hawkins, P. and Shohet, R. (1989) *Supervision in the helping professions.* Milton Keynes: Open University Press.

Haynes, C. P. A. and Naidoo, S. (1991) *Children with specific speech and language impairment. Clinics in Developmental Medicine Series.* London: MacKeith Press.

Higgin, J., Leach, F., Mann, W. and Mortimer, C. (1992) 'The advantages of a dual qualification', *Human Communication* **1**(4), 17–20.

Hoddell, S. (1995) 'Building confidence and communication', *Royal College of Speech and Language Therapists' Bulletin* **514**, 13–15.

I CAN (1987) *Language Through Reading III.* London: I CAN.

Idol, L. and West, J. F. (1987) 'Consultation in special education [Part 2]: training and practice', *Journal of Learning Disabilities* **20**, 474–94.

Idol, L. and West, J. F. (1991) 'Educational collaboration: a catalyst for effective schooling', *Intervention in School and Clinic* **27**, 70–8.

Jacklin, A. and Lacey, J. (1993) 'The integration process: a developmental model', *Support for Learning* **8**(2) 51–7.

Johnson, L. J., Pugach, M. C. and Devlin, S. (1990) 'Professional collaboration', *Teaching Exceptional Children*, Winter, 9–11.

Jordan, A. (1994) *Skills in collaborative classroom consultation.* London: Routledge.

Jowett, S. and Evans, C. (1996) *Speech and language therapy services for children.* Windsor: NFER–Nelson.

Kersner, M. (1996) 'Working together for children with SLD', *Child Language Teaching and Therapy* **12** (1), 17–28.

Kersner, M. and Stone, J. (1990) 'Survey: stress in the NHS – when the strain begins to show', *Speech Therapy in Practice* **6**(5).

Kersner, M. and Wright, J. A. (1995) 'A survey of collaborative working practices between teachers and speech and language therapists working with children with severe learning disabilities', in Kersner, M. and Peppe, S. (eds) *Work in Progress* **V** 13–23. London: University College London.

Kersner, M. and Wright, J. A. (1996) 'Collaboration between teachers and speech and language therapists working with children with severe learning disabilities (SLD): implications for professional development', *British Journal of Learning Disabilities* **24**(1), 33–7.

Knowles, W. and Masidlover, M. (1982) *The Derbyshire Language Scheme* (2nd edn). Derbyshire Education Authority.

Lacey, P. (1996) 'Supporting pupils with special educational needs', in Mills, J. (ed.) *Partnership in the primary school: working in collaboration.* London: Routledge.

Lacey, P. and Lomas, J. (1993) *Support services and the curriculum.* London: David Fulton Publishers.

Lea, J. (1970) *The Colour Pattern Scheme: a method of remedial language teaching.* Oxted: Moor House School.

Loxley, A. (1997) *Collaboration in health and welfare: working with difference.* London: Jessica Kingsley Publishers.

Lynas, W., Lewis, S. and Hopwood,V. (1997) 'Supporting the education of deaf children in mainstream schools', *The Journal of the British Association of Teachers of the Deaf* **21**(2), 41–5.

Miller, C. and Roux, J. (1997) 'Working with 11–16 year old pupils with language and communication difficulties in the mainstream school', *Child Language Teaching and Therapy* **13**(3).

Miller, C. and Wright, J. A (1995) 'Teachers of pupils with speech and language difficulties: outcomes of specialist courses', *Child Language Teaching and Therapy* **3**, 308–18.

Miller, O. and Porter, J. (1994) 'Teacher training: settling the bill', *British Journal of Special Education* **21**, 7–8.

Mills, J. (ed.) (1996) *Partnership in the primary school: working in collaboration*. London: Routledge.

Mobley, P. (1987) 'Integration in school at primary and secondary level', in Stone, J. and Kersner, M. (eds) *Language units: a review*. London: National Hospital's College of Speech Sciences.

MorganBarry, R. and Wright, J. A. (1996) 'How to recognise speech and language problems', in Kersner, M. and Wright J. A. (eds) *How to Manage Communication Problems in Young Children* (2nd edn). London: David Fulton Publishers.

Newman, S. (1996) 'Working on both sides of the fence: the effect of a dual qualification on collaborative working practice', *Child Language Teaching and Therapy* **12**(1), 39–47.

Norwich, B. (1990) *Reappraising special needs education*. London: Cassell.

Popple, J. and Wellington, W. (1996) 'Collaborative working within a psycholinguistic framework', *Child Language Teaching and Therapy* **12**(1), 60–70.

Prelock, P. A., Miller, B. L. and Reed, M. L. (1995) 'Collaborative partnerships in "a language in the classroom" program', *Language Speech and Hearing Services in Schools* **26**, 287.

Pugach, M. C. and Johnson, L. J. (1995) *Collaborative practitioners: collaborative schools*. USA: Love Publishing.

RCSLT (1996) *Communicating Quality 2* (2nd edn). London: Royal College of Speech and Language Therapists.

RCSLT (1997) *The role of the speech and language therapist in the multi-professional assessment of children with special educational needs*. London: Royal College of Speech and Language Therapists.

Regina v Harrow London Borough Council, *ex parte* M. 1996. AFASIC Newsletter, p. 4.

Reid, J., Millar, S., Tait, L., Donaldson, M. L., Dean, E. C., Thomson, G. O. B. and Grieve, R. (1996) *The role of speech and language therapists in the education of pupils with special educational needs*. Edinburgh Centre for Research in Child Development.

Rinaldi, W. (1992) *Social Use of Language Programme* Windsor: NFER–Nelson.

Roberts, V. Z. (1994) 'Conflict and collaboration: managing intergroup relations', in Obholzer, A. and Roberts, V. Z. (eds) *The unconscious at work*. London: Routledge.

Roux, J. (1996) 'Working collaboratively with teachers: supporting the newly qualified speech and language therapist in a mainstream school', *Child Language Teaching and Therapy* **12**(1), 48–59.

Sandow, S., Stafford, D. and Stafford, P. (1987) *An agreed understanding? Parent professional communication and the 1981 Education Act.* Windsor: NFER–Nelson.

Sanger, D. D., Hux, K. and Griess, K. (1995) 'Educators' opinions about speech-language pathology services in schools', *Language Speech and Hearing Services in Schools* **26**, 75–86.

SENTC (1996) 'Professional development to meet special educational needs'. Report to the Department for Education and Employment. Special Educational Needs Training Consortium.

Shaw, L., Luscombe, M. and Ostime, J. (1996) 'Collaborative working in the development of a school based speech and language therapy service'. Caring to Communicate. Proceedings of the Golden Jubilee Conference, Royal College of Speech and Language Therapists, 330–42.

Sherif, M. (1966) *Group conflict and co-operation.* London: Routledge and Kegan Paul.

Snowling, M. and Stackhouse, J. (eds) (1996) *Dyslexia, speech and language: a practitioner's handbook.* London: Whurr Publishers.

Stackhouse, J. (1996) 'Speech, spelling and reading: who is at risk and why?', in Snowling, M. and Stackhouse, J. (eds) *Dyslexia, speech and language: a practitioner's handbook.* London: Whurr Publishers.

Stackhouse, J. and Wells, B. (1997) *Children's speech and literacy difficulties: a psycholinguistic framework.* London: Whurr Publishers.

Tannen, D. and Wallet, C. (1986) 'Medical professionals and parents: a linguistic analysis of communication across contexts', *Language in Society* **15**, 295–312.

Urwin, S., Cook, J. and Kelly, K. (1988) 'Pre-school language intervention: a follow-up study', *Child Care Health and Development* **14**, 127–46.

Wade, B. and Moore, M. (1992) *Patterns of educational integration: international perspectives on mainstreaming children with special educational needs.* Wallingford: Triangle Books.

Webster, A. and McConnell, C. (1987) *Speech and language difficulties in children.* London: Cassell.

Wintgens, A. (1996) 'Links between emotional/behavioural problems and communication difficulties', in Kersner, M. and Wright, J. A. (eds) *How to Manage Communication Problems in Young Children* (2nd edn). London: David Fulton Publishers.

Winyard, S. (1996) 'The development of communication – speech and language acquisition', in Kersner, M. and Wright, J. A. (eds) *How to Manage Communication Problems in Young Children* (2nd edn). London: David Fulton Publishers.

Withey, C. (1991) 'Creating an environment to facilitate communication growth within a language unit', *Child Language Teaching and Therapy* **7**(2), 115–26.

Wright, J. A. (1992) 'Collaboration between teachers and speech therapists with language impaired children', in Fletcher, P. and Hall, D. (eds) *Specific speech and language disorders in children.* London: Whurr Publishers.

Wright, J. A. (1994) 'Collaboration between therapists and teachers.' Unpublished PhD thesis. University of London.

Wright, J. A. (1995) 'Provision for children with communiation difficulties', in Lunt, I., Norwich, B. and Varma, V. (eds) *Psychology and education for special needs: recent developments and future directions.* Aldershot: Ashgate Publishing.

Wright, J. A. (1996) 'Teachers and therapists: the evolution of a partnership', *Child Language Teaching and Therapy* **12**(1), 3–17.

Wrynne, T. (1986) 'Links, schemes and integration – the Dawn House experience', in *Advances in working with language disordered children.* Conference Paper. London: ICAA.

Index